S0-AVG-396

VIRGINIA S. CARR

TOYBOX TALES

STORIES OF OLD DOLLS AND TOYS PHOTOGRAPHED IN CHARMING SETTINGS

Photography by Edward H. Leland

PRUETT PUBLISHING COMPANY
Boulder, Colorado

First Edition
1 2 3 4 5 6 7 8 9

Printed in the United States of America

Library of Congress Cataloging in Publication Data

Carr, Virginia S., 1918-
"Toybox Tales".

Bibliography: p.
Includes index.
1. Dolls 2.Toys. I. Title.
NK4893.C371982 688.7'2 82-455
ISBN 0-87108-623-9 AACR2

Foreword

Toybox Tales is a collection of stories about dolls and toys, written in narrative style, but with the inclusion of documentary information to assist in the recognition and identification of these precious old toys. The main objective of this book is to record for the future some nostalgic memories of our life-styles as they once were.

Dolls have served as models in many photographs to enact a particular scene or to carry out the story line. In addition, many favorite old toys for boys are pictured and described throughout the book.

Writing this book served to recall many happy memories of my childhood. It is my hope that it will be read with equal pleasure by both men and women, who will care enough to share it with their children, thus keeping alive many otherwise forgotten traditions.

With best regards,

Virginia Carr

Acknowledgements and Credits

Several people inspired me to complete *Toybox Tales*. I wish to thank everyone who encouraged me to write this book, with special appreciation to my husband, Guy, for being patient and supportive; and to my children, Bonnie and John, for understanding what I set out to do and urging me to finish it. I could not have assembled the many things needed in our photo settings without the unfailing help of my friend, Jo Heinz, and the assistance and talents of Kay Johnson, Mabel Oliphant, and Helen Smith.

Many others graciously loaned or gave me dolls, toys, or accessories. My thanks to each of them for sharing these items with all of us:

Mildred Beckwith
Rick Beckwith
Margaret Chipman
Esther Day
Pauly Deem
Donna Dorn
Susan Dorn
Shirlee Glass
Barbara Gray
Anne Hardesty
George Holte
Lola Johnson
Lynn Johnson
Irma Kleen
Jim Mains
Jocelyn Mann
Nora Montgomery
Hiro Murakami
Helen Rink
Bob Smith
Toddy Thompson
Hugh Van Male
Margaret White
Warren Yarroll

I wish also to acknowledge Ed Leland's artistic ideas of perfection which resulted in beautiful photography, and Don Paist's valuable editorial assistance.

Contents

Photos 1 & 2: On Monday morning, Dora is hard at work washing clothes. She is a 21-inch, brown-haired doll with a bisque head.

1. Woman's Work is Never Done

Many years ago, before laundry equipment became so sophisticated and automatic, the family laundry was an awesome weekly task, and a considerable amount of time was involved in accomplishing the washing and ironing each week. For this reason, it was customary and practical for most housewives to set aside Monday to do the weekly washing, Tuesday to iron the clothes, Wednesday to do the mending, and so on.

Monday

Dora is hard at work on a warm summer morning, operating the doll-size wooden washing machine which had to be cranked by hand. The washer had to be filled with buckets of hot water carried from the old wood-burning stove, and shavings of homemade lye soap formed the hot, bubbly suds. The clothes were washed and lifted out of the washer, boiled in a copper boiler on the stove, then the hot clothes were lifted out with a big broomstick and swirled around in a tub of rinse water. After the first layer of soapsuds was rinsed away, the clothes would go into still another tub of water to which some "bluing" was added, for would you believe—*bluing* was put in to make the *white* clothes look *whiter*! Now wasn't that strange? Then each garment was carefully guided through a set of rubber wringer rolls to squeeze out the excess water, as shown at the right in the photograph. This is a salesman's sample from the early 1900s *Horseshoe Brand*, made by the American Wringer Company of New York. It is 6 inches wide and 4-½ inches tall.

In still another process, many of the garments would be submerged for a third time in a pan of hot starch, then wrung out and hung on the clothesline with wooden clothespins and left to flap and dry in the breeze. However, if it was raining, the clothes would be hung on a line in the kitchen as shown here.

The first picture shows the washer, which was made around 1900, with lid closed, in operation, and the next picture shows the working part, or agitator, inside the washer.

Dora is a 21-inch, brown-haired doll, unmarked except for 199 on the back of her neck. She has a bisque head on composition body, with ball-jointed arms and legs. Ball-jointed means that the doll's arms are joined at the wrists and elbows by a round wooden ball which allows the hand to be turned and the elbow to move up and down. In the same manner, the knees are more easily moved by this type of construction. A composition body was made in several ways, sometimes of a papier-mache base, and sometimes from sawdust or wood pulp, glue and water. Some doll makers formed the bodies from grey paper, and glued the fronts and backs together, then applied the socket for the ball-jointed articulation. The body was then painted, sanded, and several more coats of paint added, and finally, a coat of varnish was applied to complete its shiny finish.

Dora was probably made in Germany before 1890, since, after that date, the law required that the country of origin be shown on doll imports. She wears a long, grey printed cotton housedress, drab in color, but purposely chosen because it didn't show soil.

In *Photo 3*, Barbara is laboring over still another chore which was part of the weekly laundry routine, and in some cases, even done on a daily basis for large families. Someone had to bend over a metal (or glass) washboard and vigorously scrub some garments like overalls, which were heavily soiled, in order to loosen the dirt before placing them in the washing machine; or to lightly hand wash the delicate things such as gloves and handkerchiefs. Barbara is a 32-inch doll with a bisque head, made around 1910 by Armand Marseille, on a composition body with ball-jointed wooden arms and legs, made by Max Handwerck who specialized in making doll bodies. Armand Marseille (pronounced MARSAY), though his name is of French origin, actually came from Russia, and had a factory in Koppelsdorf, Germany, which he started in 1865. He produced probably the largest quantity of bisque doll heads of anyone in the doll industry.

Barbara has large, blue, glass eyes that sleep, an open mouth with four teeth, and a blonde wig of corkscrew curls. She is dressed in a white batiste dress, with a blue cotton apron made from quilt blocks, and she wears a white mobcap to keep her curls nice while she does her housework.

The wicker clothes hamper at left is a salesman's sample made in the U.S.A. in 1932.

Tuesday

Now it is Tuesday, and Ella Mae is ironing the clothes, which were washed and dried on Monday and "dampened down," as we used to say, meaning that each piece of clothing, and especially the starched pieces, had to be sprinkled quite thoroughly with water and rolled up so the moisture would be well distributed through the garment. Ella Mae can then iron out all the wrinkles from the dresses and undergarments, shirts, linens, and other items and lay them over the drying rack (called a clotheshorse) to thoroughly dry before being folded and placed in bureau drawers. The rack, as shown here, was also used to dry the laundry on bad days when the clothes could not be hung outdoors on the line. The toy clotheshorse and ironing board were made around 1914. Irons were not electrically heated then. They were called "sad irons" and had to be heated on the old cookstove in the kitchen. This toy iron dates back to the 1800s. Irons were heavy to lift, and women were very tired when they finished the chore of ironing.

Ella Mae is a 24-inch doll with a bisque head, a brown mohair wig, and a ball-jointed composition body, made in 1906 by Heinrich Handwerck, another well-known German doll manufacturer (brother of Max Handwerck), who specialized in making doll bodies, as well as heads. Ella Mae wears a long housedress of dark brown, and her brown mohair wig is braided and wrapped around her head.

Photo 3: Seen here using a washboard to gently handwash a delicate handkerchief, Barbara is 32 inches tall, and her bisque head was made in Germany by Armand Marseille, who produced probably the largest number of bisque doll heads in the doll industry.

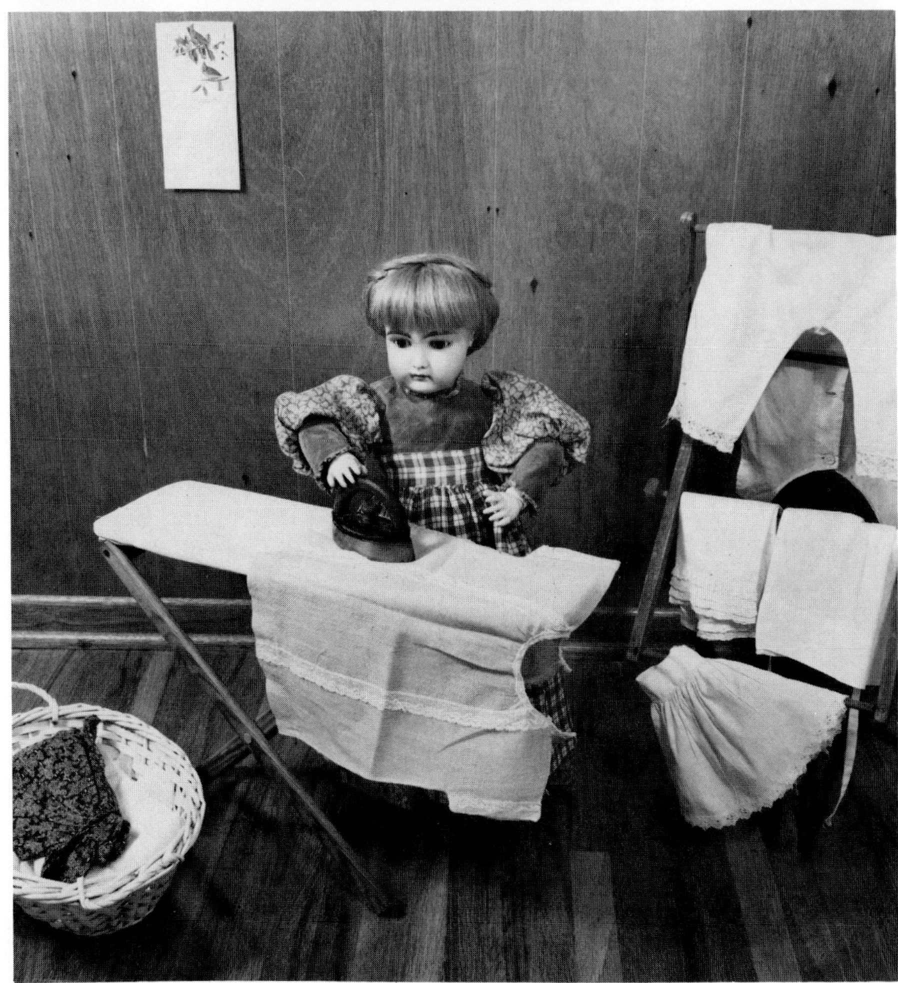

Photo 4: It's Tuesday, and Ella Mae is ironing the clothes and laying them over the clotheshorse to thoroughly dry. She was made in 1906 by Heinrich Handwerck.

Photo 5: Wednesday is the time for doing the weekly mending and sewing chores, and Vera is working at the sewing machine, while Kathleen is doing some embroidery on a doily. Both dolls were made in Germany.

Photo 6: Thursday is marketing day, and Sally and Meg are returning home with their baskets full of groceries. They are both Florodora dolls, 32 inches tall, and made by Armand Marseille around 1915.

Wednesday

On Wednesday, the ladies of the household liked to sit down in a sunny corner of the house, most likely the kitchen or living room, to do the weekly mending and sewing tasks. Some of the more wealthy families had a separate "sewing" room just for this purpose, which was equipped with a sewing machine, an ironing board for pressing, and helpful household tools. Wednesday was a good day to do one's mending because the ironing chore performed on Tuesday always revealed little rips and tears in garments which needed to be "caught" with a needle, or even sewn with sturdier seams on the sewing machine. It was also a good day to relax with some embroidery work in one's lap, after a strenuous two days of washing and ironing. There was often a cat at their feet, purring with contentment, yet hoping to have its neck stroked as a reward for having caught some mice in the pantry.

Vera is sitting at the toy sewing machine (made in early 1900s in Germany), stitching a new aqua taffeta coat, while Kathleen sits leisurely in a rocking chair, with an embroidery hoop and floss on her lap, doing fancy stitches on a doily.

Vera is a 14-inch doll with a bisque head, marked "2015 Made in Germany" by J. D. Kestner around 1912. The Kestner firm was one of the foremost German doll designers from about 1860 on, and it was known for the excellent quality of dolls that it produced. The faces were very carefully painted in soft detail, and the eyes were so pretty, they almost looked real. Vera's head is slightly turned on the shoulder plate, with a kid body, composition legs, and bisque lower arms. She has a blonde wig of human hair, pretty blue eyes, and is dressed in white cotton with a lovely lace Bertha collar and lace panels in the full skirt. The waistline is emphasized by a blue, moire taffeta ribbon sash.

Kathleen is also a 14-inch doll with a bisque head on a kid and cloth body, made in Germany in 1915 by Armand Marseille. She has a wig of brown mohair, blue sleep eyes, and is dressed in a blue, sprigged afternoon dress of lawn, with full tiered skirt, and blue velvet ribbon sash.

The cat is white bisque, made in Germany around 1910.

Thursday

Thursday was marketing day, and in *Photo* 6 we see Sally and Meg with their baskets over their arms, returning from the store, where they have done their shopping. They are chatting before separating to go into their own houses. The need for groceries and other items offers them an opportunity to get some fresh air and a bit of exercise, as well as a chance to catch up on the latest "goings on" in the neighborhood.

Sally and Meg are both Florodora dolls, 22 inches tall, made by Armand Marseille around 1915, with bisque heads, brown mohair wigs, kid bodies, and bisque arms and legs. Sally has brown eyes, and Meg's are blue. Sally is dressed in a street-length, yellow brocade material with a bustle in the back, trimmed in blue velvet ribbon and eyelet lace. Her off-the-face hat is of matching material, and is trimmed with a blue ostrich plume and flowers.

Photo 7: Friday is cleaning day, and Iris is pushing the carpet sweeper while Barbara (also seen in Photo 3) is using the feather duster. Iris was made by J. D. Kestner in 1915.

Meg wears a dotted Swiss street-length dress of tan with black dots, black lace trim, and an antique jet pin at the neckline. She wears an Irish crocheted lace cap on her head. Both are carrying wicker market baskets filled with their purchases of fish, bread, apples, and a small doll from the toy shop.

Friday

Friday was always cleaning day, and in *Photo 7* Iris is pushing the carpet sweeper over the rugs, and Barbara has a feather duster in her hand. Iris is a 33-inch doll marked "No. 214 JDK", made by J. D. Kestner in 1915, with a bisque head and a composition body. She wears a white lawn dress which is protected by a pink gingham apron, and a bandana over her hair. Barbara is the 32-inch doll who is washing clothes on the washboard in *Photo 3*. She wears a kerchief over her curls to keep dust out of her hair while dusting a toy corner cupboard, with pretty pieces of china and miniature figurines on its shelves. The carpet sweeper is an antique, toy-size Bissell "Little Jewel" made around 1910, a complete miniature of the regular size ones which were in use before electric vacuum sweepers came into being.

Photo 8: On Saturday morning, Miss Carrie takes an angel food cake out of the woodburning stove. She is 17 inches tall and her head is made of tin.

Saturday

Saturday was the weekly baking day. Since families were rather large in those days, and it was quite a job to fire up the old cookstove to the right temperature, the lady of the house liked to do all her baking at one time; therefore, she baked as many things as possible while the oven was hot enough to do so.

In *Photo 8* Miss Carrie is standing near the stove, beaming with pride at the angel food cake she has just taken out of the oven. The old toy version of a wood-burning cookstove, which was manufactured near the turn of the century, is made of cast iron. It is 14 inches high and 18 inches long. The stove lids lift out; it has a warming oven at the top and a water reservoir at one side; the little pans and skillets are also made of iron, all of which are exact replicas of what grownups cooked with at that time. The stove has the name "RIVAL" on the oven door.

No kitchen at that time would have been complete without a coal bucket, broom, and dustpan near the stove, for the floor was in constant need of being swept because of wood ash and soot which floated away from the fire. The broom was a vital baking aid in itself, for women used to pull a straw from the broom and insert the clean end of it through the center of their cakes to see if they were done.

The toy cupboard is filled with dishes, as well as cooking utensils and mixing bowls, and a doll-size cannister set can be seen on the lower shelf with tiny china containers marked "COFFEE," "SUGAR," "TEA," "CINNAMON," etc. The cupboard was handmade about 1910 by a father for his daughter's Christmas present.

Carrie is a lady doll, 17 inches tall, with a metal head which was made by Juno near the turn of the century. She has a pretty painted face and molded, wavy, honey-colored hair. Her tin head has been sewn to a cloth body with leather arms and stitched fingers, cloth legs, and leather boots on her feet. She is wearing a striped cotton dress and apron until she finishes her baking and tidies up the kitchen. Then she will change to her "good" dress before going out for the afternoon.

2. Sunday at the Ice Cream Social

The ice cream social, usually held on the church lawn around the turn of the century, was one of the highlights of the summer season. No one wanted to miss this great event, which always happened on one of the hottest summer days. There was no such thing as air conditioning then, nor even an electric fan. Instead, the ladies held a cardboard fan in their hands and rapidly waved it in an effort to cool their feverish brows.

There was much preparation for days ahead of this big event, as the ladies baked mouth-watering devil's food or light angel food cakes in their old cookstoves. On the morning of the social, they would have to hand-crank the ice cream freezers until their arms would ache, in order to whip up the cold and tasty ice cream.

This little family of dolls in *Photo 9* is anxiously waiting to be taken to the social. They have been counting the days until time to go—now, at last, they are all dressed up in their Sunday best, for they expect to see many of their friends. The girls hope for admiring glances from one of their favorite boy dolls.

Marybelle and Mibs are seated opposite one another on the toy lawn swing like people used to have in their yards. It would sway back and forth in a pleasing manner, stirring up a bit of a breeze, as well as affording the young ladies a chance to whisper and gossip a little. There was a slatted floor in the swing which kept its passenger's feet up off the ground. The swing was often placed near a lilac bush which offered a lovely fragrance, as well as a bit of welcome shade from the sun. This one is red enameled, 20-½ inches high, with a 17-inch spread, 12-½ inches wide, and was made in 1914.

Marybelle, the doll seated on the left side of the swing, is an all-wood doll patented in 1911 by A. Schoenhut & Company. Albert Schoenhut was born in Germany in 1850, came to America in 1867, and started his toy factory in 1872. These dolls were labeled "All-Wood Perfection Art Dolls," and because of their special spring-jointed bodies, they could be placed in any position with hands high, legs kicking, or many other poses. They had beautiful, oil-painted faces, and their feet were made with two holes in the soles which fit a special stand. Marybelle is 15 inches tall, with painted blue eyes. Her wig of blonde mohair may or may not be original to the doll. She was probably made around 1914. She wears a blue and white tiny checked cotton gingham dress with horizontal tucks and white lace insertion. She is trying to coax a cooling breeze with her palm leaf fan.

"Mibs," on the right side of the swing, is a 16-inch doll designed by Hazel Drukker and made by Louis Amberg in 1922 with a painted composition head and limbs, cork-stuffed body, wearing a dress of red and white check cotton with eyelet beading, laced with red satin ribbon. Originally she wore a tag which read "Please love me, I'm Mibs."

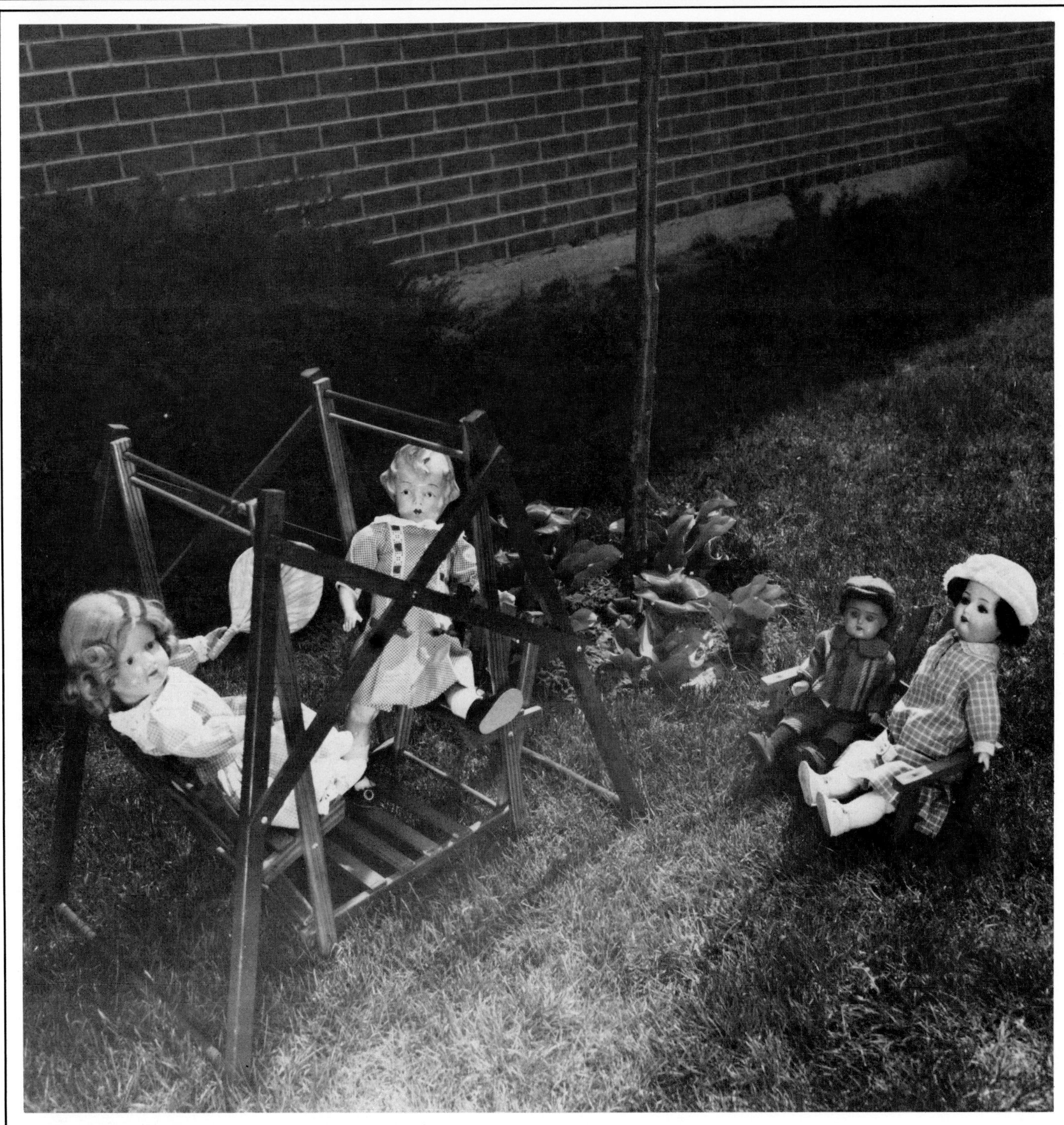

Photo 9: On a hot, summer day this little family of dolls is waiting to be taken to the ice cream social. Sitting in the lawn swing, Marybelle (left) is an all-wood doll with a spring-jointed body, and "Mibs" was made by Louis Amberg in 1922. On the wooden lawn chair sit Beatrice and her brother Donald; she was made in Germany in 1905; he has a shiny pottery head and was made during the first decade of this century.

Photo 10: (From left to right) *meet Carolyn, Patricia, Louella and Adeline; they are all German-made except for Patricia who was made in France, probably before 1890. They sit in canvas lawn chairs which are handmade miniatures of chairs advertised in the Sears 1908 Catalogue.*

Sitting in the wooden lawn duet chair are Beatrice and her little brother, Donald. Beatrice is a 14-inch doll with a bisque head on a composition body, made by Wagner Zetzsche, in Germany, in about 1905. She has a brown mohair wig, blue eyes, and is dressed in grey and white gingham with a hat to match.

Donald is an 11-inch, unmarked boy doll made around 1900 to 1910, with a shiny pottery head, blue eyes, wooden upper arms and legs, and composition lower legs, and he is dressed in a brown wool boy's suit and cap, dark stockings, and brown laced shoes. Being a typical boy, it is very difficult for Donald to sit still, stay clean, and "mind his manners." Beatrice must keep her eye on him.

In *Photo 10*, at the far left, in the striped canvas sling chair is Carolyn, a brown-eyed doll with a bisque head and a composition body, and dressed in pale blue and white striped silk and a red straw hat on her brown mohair wig. Dangling from her wrist is a miniature clown. She was made by Kestner in Germany around 1900 to 1915.

Sitting in the wicker chair next to Carolyn is Patricia, a 14-inch tall doll with a bisque head, blue eyes, and a composition body, and dressed in peach-colored satin, a white crocheted hat on a blonde mohair wig, and wearing striped stockings with black shoes. She is an unmarked French type, age unknown, but possibly made before 1890. She carries a gold mesh purse, which was an important fashion accessory around 1910.

In the wicker chair next to Patricia is Louella, a 14-inch Kestner marked "161," made around 1910, with a bisque head, a blonde mohair wig, brown eyes, and a composition body, and dressed in a pink satin dress with a pleated skirt and lace collar and cuffs. She wears unusual chamois-colored boots and holds a tortoise shell fan in her hand.

At the far right is Adeline, another 14-inch German bisque head on a composition body marked "Catterfeld Fabrikpuppen," made around 1912, with blue eyes, and dressed in a provincial costume of black skirt and a white blouse, and wearing her blonde mohair wig in braids. She has an open-work, lacey ivory fan on her lap.

The wicker table and chairs are dark brown, from about 1910; the doll-size, cut-glass pitcher and glasses are of about the same era. The iron bulldog in the foreground is from the early 1900s.

The canvas-type lawn chairs are handmade by Mabel Oliphant, and are miniatures of the original old chairs which were advertised in the *Sears 1908 Catalogue* in this manner.

THE CHICAGO FOLDING PORCH CHAIR, 78¢

The Chicago porch chair, made of wood frame with denim body. All joints riveted and may be folded when not in use. Back may be adjusted to various angles for comfort. All have arm rests and high back, are easily carried about and save the household furniure.
Price 78¢

From the price alone, one can readily tell that the catalogue is quite out-of-date.

3. Action Toys for Boys

Ralph appears to be hard at work, in *Photos 11* and *12*, shoveling sand into his wooden bucket as it trickles from the bed of the dump truck onto the cement. However, the plain truth is that he enjoys what he is doing, just as little boys used to back in 1925 when these toys were new. The 26-inch dump truck is all metal, a combination of iron and tin, and was once painted a shiny black with red wheels. Fragments of a decal on the side tell us that it was made by Keystone Manufacturing Company of Boston, Massachusetts and patented December 15, 1925. The crank at the front is like the one with which all cars and trucks were equipped at this time, for if the motor failed to turn over, it had to be cranked in order to start. A little lever beneath the truck, operated by a simple twist of the wrist, will make the truck bed gradually rise at the end nearest the cab, so as to free its contents to pour out onto the ground. By reversing the crank, one can restore the truck bed to its level position for reloading. This was an operation which was repeated over and over again by little boys pretending to be truck drivers; and to make the whole thing seem even more realistic, they would make a sputtering noise with their lips which sounded so much like truck motors, it sent many a mother to the window to see what was whizzing by!

The steam shovel is of the same period, 1910 to 1925, one of the "Buddy L" line quality toys made by Moline Pressed Steel Company of Moline, Illinois. It is also made of iron and tin, and the overall length of its cab and derrick (or crane) is 21 inches. It, too, has a mechanical device which allows one to raise or lower the bucket and to accurately position it to dig into a hill of sand or dirt and take a healthy bite out of it before being swung around to the spot where it will dramatically release its contents. This one was a replica of the powerful steam shovel which was once made in Marion, Ohio, during the early 1900s at the Marion Steam Shovel Company.

Ralph is a 14-inch doll made by Gebruder Heubach around 1909, with a bisque head and a mohair wig, blue sleep eyes, a laughing open mouth with two lower teeth, and a jointed composition body. He is marked on the back of his neck with the sunburst Heubach mark, and "Germany." Ralph is dressed in black knee britches and white pique shirt, black socks, and red leather shoes with two buttons.

Photo 13 shows a group of mechanical tin toys which delighted both boys and girls in the late 1920s and early 30s. There was action aplenty in each of these attractively decorated toys.

Singing birds have been imitated for centuries. A Parisian named Robert Robin made a life-size singing canary for Marie Antoinette in a beautiful gilded cage with a clock base. The clock was set so that the canary sang every hour. Another one in 1752 was enclosed in a gold snuffbox so that when the lid was opened, the

Photos 11 & 12: Ralph is a 14-inch doll made by Gebruder Heubach around 1909. The toy dump truck, 26 inches long, was made in 1925, and the steam shovel dates from 1910–1925.

bird would spring up and start singing. These became very popular and were considered sort of an adult "toy" and were much in demand. They were made both in France and Switzerland. Some were so tiny, they were only a few inches high, yet the bird would still pop up from the box. Needless to say, these were quite expensive.

In the 1920s, some German firms made less expensive singing birds, with a true imitation of the songs of the goldfinch, warbler, blackbird, canary, or nightingale. The one pictured here is an example in fine condition. Made of tin, with a clockwork mechanism, it is brightly painted with gaily colored plumage, and when wound, its wings flap and it sings a shrill but melodious tune.

The lithographed, tin ski toy was made in the U.S.A. by J. Chein & Company during the early '30s. It is basically a 2-piece body with a front and back fastened together in the middle, with arms fastened at the shoulders, and the entire figure mounted on skis with invisible wheels underneath. When its clock mechanism is wound by the key at the right side, the skier moves forward rapidly on his skis, lifting his ski poles up and down as he "skis" along. This is one of many such mechanical toys that was fun to play with on the floor, on one's hands and knees.

The tin, lithographed parade drummer was made in the United States approximately in 1924, and features a drummer dressed in uniform, beating on a huge bass drum. Printed in large letters around the edge of the drum is "Let the Drummer Boy Play While You Swing and Sway." When wound with the key on the side, the figure struts along, beats the drum, and marches in parade step, while moving his head up and down with the beat of the drum.

The cat in the foreground is metal, covered with black felt, with a tin ball in his paws. This toy was made in Germany in the early 1900s, and has invisible wheels beneath it. When wound by its key, it scurries across the floor, chasing the ball.

The other figure is also metal, covered with black felt, and was made in Germany about the same time as the cat. It is that of a man dressed in a black suit, and when wound, he brings his arms up and over his head swinging the celluloid doll up high, then back down to the floor, in the same manner as a father might entertain his little daughter.

The large iron piece at the back of the picture was made in the late nineteenth century; it is a heavy, cast iron toy sleigh pulled by two reindeer and guided by Santa Claus, who is surrounded by many presents for little boys and girls. These are painted various colors of red, blue, black, etc, and Santa himself is in his usual red suit. The overall length of this toy is 12 inches, and it is 6 inches high. A small wheel between the reindeer and a cord tied to the front enabled a child to pull it along, and no doubt it was even pulled through the snow. Through the years, it has shed much of its original paint.

Photo 13: Mechanical tin toys such as these delighted boys and girls in the late 1920s and early 1930s.

4. Clowning Around

It is generally agreed among all professional clowns that, first and foremost, the philosophy behind being a clown is to give of yourself to other people, to make them laugh and be happy. Theirs is an art that is special, the art of making people forget their cares and for a time, at least, to laugh at someone willing to act the fool and ridicule himself.

A revealing bit of prose, describing a clown's philosophy, is quoted here (author unknown):

A Clown's Prayer

Dear Lord, help me to create more laughter than tears, disperse more happiness than gloom, spread more cheer than despair.

Never let me grow so big that I fail to see the wonder in the eyes of a child or the twinkle in the eyes of the aged.

Never let me forget that I am a clown . . . that my work is to cheer people up, make them happy, and allow them to laugh; to forget momentarily all the unpleasant things in their lives.

Never let me acquire financial success to the point where I will discontinue calling upon my Creator in the hour of my need or acknowledging Him in my hours of plenty. Amen.

Harlequin clowns date back in French history to 1100 A.D. Harlequins always wore a mask and colorful tights, performing in pantomime.

Pierrot, another type of clown, also performed in French pantomime, wearing white makeup and a white clown suit. He was an emotional type who usually pretended to hide great sadness beneath his comic mask.

Today's whiteface clowns are a direct influence from the Harlequins and Pierrot comedians and jesters of the Middle Ages. Their eyebrows, noses, and mouths are usually painted in black and red makeup. If the features are made to look overly large, the face is called "grotesque whiteface." The whiteface clown dresses in pretty silks and satins, and is the leader in a group of clowns, the one who gets the others into trouble, but takes none of the blame.

The august clown wears the outlandish costumes with baggy pants, too-large shoes, smokes very large cigars, and his base makeup is pink or reddish, rather than white. His oversized features are painted in red or black. This type of clown is a fun-loving but clumsy behaving comic—the slapstick comedian.

Character clowns are those who play a specific role, such as the Keystone Cop, the tramp, or the juggler, and usually they do a solo act in the spotlight, depicting that particular character.

Charlie Chaplin was classified not only as an actor of great renown, but as a clown as well. He once described the philosophy

Photo 14: (Clockwise from left) *a lady clown doll, 11 inches tall, an original by De Nicola; Smiley whose expression can be changed from a grin to a frown by a special mechanism; Emmett Kelly, a 15-inch-tall Willie the Clown doll; and a Schoenhut carved wooden clown, made in 1905.*

behind his mode of dress: "The costume helps me to express my conception of the average man, of myself. The derby, too small, is striving for dignity. The mustache is vanity. The tightly-buttoned coat and the stick and his whole manner are a gesture towards gallantry and dash."

One of the most famous and highly respected of all clowns was the late Emmett Kelly, the hobo clown. He started his circus career as a trapeze artist in the 1920s, doubling as a whiteface clown. Eventually, he developed his character of "Weary Willie," the sad-faced clown. He never changed his expression, never laughed or talked, but still he won the love of all who saw him silently perform.

In *Photo 14*, we see a group of four clown dolls, all different, but each with its own special appeal. At far right is Emmett Kelly, a 15-inch Willie the Clown doll, with painted vinyl head, hands, and feet, and a vinyl-stuffed body. It is a Baby Barry Toy made in New York. His hobo outfit is typical of what Emmett always wore as a performing clown. In his book *Clown*, Emmett Kelly describes himself this way: "I am a sad, ragged little guy who is very serious about everything he attempts—no matter how futile or how foolish it appears to be. I am the hobo who found out the hard way that the deck is stacked, the dice 'frozen,' the race fixed, and the wheel crooked, but there is always present that one, tiny, forlorn spark of hope still glimmering in his soul which makes him keep on trying."

At far left is a lady clown doll, 11 inches tall, an original by De Nicola, from the Craft & Folk Art Museum in California. She is

Photo 15: The two standing dolls, 18 inches tall, were made by EFFanBEE Doll Company, and sitting between them is an 18-inch-tall Pierrot, made in Japan.

made from painted composition, with a flaming red wig, and is dressed in a two-tone polka-dot clown suit.

The fat-faced clown toy in the rocking chair is 14-inch "Smiley" with a hard plastic head with painted features, white-gloved hands, and his cloth-stuffed body forms his clothes. His facial expression can be changed from a grin to a frown by a special little mechanism.

In the foreground of *Photo 14* is an old Schoenhut carved wooden clown, 7 inches tall, made in 1905 by the Schoenhut Company. It is still in its original clown suit, and the hands are shaped to grip a ladder. This was one of the pieces in the elaborate Schoenhut circus.

In *Photo 15*, the three clown dolls are all commercially made. The one in the center is an 18-inch Pierrot, made in Japan, with an intriguing porcelain face with a tear on its cheek. It is dressed in a black velvet and gold metallic cloth clown suit with two red pompons down the front, and a wide ruffle at the neck. A music box, which is concealed beneath the clothes, plays "Stardust." The chubby boy and girl clowns flanking Pierrot are made by EFFanBEE Doll Company from an original design by Faith Wick. They are 18 inches tall with whiteface clown makeup and sleep eyes, dressed in red and white coordinated outfits.

Photo 16 shows a matching pair of boy and girl clowns which are one-of-a-kind originals. Sandy, the boy clown, is dressed in red corduroy pants edged with bright floral trim and a long flowered coat with a huge red satin bow tie. Candy, the girl clown, is dressed to match, in a red corduroy redingote over a floral outfit, with a wide, red satin ruffle at the neck. Both dolls have yellow yarn wigs and carved wooden white-gloved hands, and both are wearing enormous clown shoes. These dolls were carved by Robert J. Smith, and painted and dressed by his daughter, Candy Cebula. The whimsical trapeze clown in the center was also carved and painted by Bob Smith, and is balanced on a metal lever. When the clown is turned one complete circle on the wooden bars, he will continue to revolve time after time until he finally comes to a stop at the other end.

Photo 16: Matching boy and girl clowns, carved by Robert J. Smith of Colorado, and painted and dressed by his daugher, Candy Cebula. Smith also carved the trapeze clown.

5. Sleeping Beauty

Ethel lives in a large, old ten-room Victorian house in San Francisco. She has spent a strenuous day, dusting the downstairs parlor, the "sitting room," and the dining room. It is mid-afternoon, and she is lying in bed in one of the five upstairs bedrooms, about to take a much needed rest for an hour or so. Ethel is an 11-inch china head doll with china arms and legs, on a cloth body.

China head dolls were made of glazed porcelain and had a naturally shiny appearance, as compared to bisque, which was made from unglazed ceramics. China heads were made as early as 1750, and can be dated fairly accurately by their hair styles. Most of the more elaborate china heads go back to about 1840 or 1850. Those most commonly found were called "lowbrows," which was not a reflection on the doll, but simply described the hairstyle which was wavy and which fell low over the forehead. Most china head dolls consisted of a china head, arms, and legs, and a body usually made from cloth and stuffed with sawdust; sometimes a peg wooden body was used. The finer china heads are distinguished by such things as brush marks at the hairline, red dots in the corners of the eyes, and a red line over the eyes. While the majority of china head dolls were ladies, there were also molds of children and a few men. The hair on most china heads was shiny black, but from 1880 to 1900, blondes were produced in large quantities.

Ethel is a "Pet Name China" made in 1905 in Germany by Butler Brothers, who owned the models used for making the heads. This doll had a girl's name fired in gold across the front of the shoulder plate and a collar and bow design in gold, which resembled the bodice of a dress. The name which can barely be seen in the picture is (of course) "ETHEL." Other names commonly found on the Pet Name China were Agnes, Bertha, Dorothy, Helen, Mabel, and Marion.

Ethel's old metal bed was made around the turn of the century, and is collapsible for storage. The sheets and pillow case are edged in old crocheted lace, and the green wool comforter knotted with green yarn is typical of the kind of bed covers used at that time.

The toy wooden dresser, with wooden knobs on the drawers, was handmade in 1910. An oval double picture frame with pearl and amethyst decoration sits on the top level of smaller drawers, and a miniature single gold picture frame sits on the lower level. A mirror hangs above the dresser. The bottom drawer of the dresser stands open, revealing crisply pressed linen dresser scarves and bedding.

Beulah, standing at the right, is holding the dress which Ethel will put on when she awakens from her nap. Beulah is a 13-inch china head that was manufactured in 1885 in Germany, with shiny black hair and brush marks at the hairline, china arms and legs, and a cloth body. She is dressed in a floor-length dress with white bodice, a blue-flowered, cotton voile full skirt with ruffle

at the hem, over which she wears a fancy white organdy apron. The dress in her arms is lavender and gold printed voile, with pin tucks in the skirt, and trimmed in lavender ribbons, to be worn over a white batiste blouse.

Beside Ethel's bed is a doll-size bedside table with a lace doily, a miniature alarm clock, and a tiny kerosine lamp. An oval crocheted rug is placed near the bed, so she won't have to step out on the cold bare floors.

Soon the alarm will ring, Ethel will jump to the floor, light the lamp, and dress for dinner, which is being prepared by her sisters downstairs in the big, old kitchen.

Photo 17: "Ethel," who is sleeping, and Beulah are German-made dolls with shiny china heads; Ethel dates from 1905 and Beulah from 1885.

6. Midsummer Evening on the Old Front Porch

In 1913, an American doll manufacturer called EFFanBEE Company (which stood for Fleischaker & Baum) began doing business, making both composition heads and cloth bodies, and by 1923 they introduced one of their most successful dolls, called "Bubbles." Shown here is a 25-inch Bubbles, the largest they made, with composition, stationary head with a long shoulder plate, cloth body, and composition arms and legs jointed at the shoulder and hip. The distingiushing feature of this doll is that her left forefinger was shaped and directed so that it would fit into her mouth. This delighted all the little girls who owned one, but in addition, Bubbles was most appealing because of her chubby, rosy cheeks with dimples, open mouth with two teeth, and large, laughing, blue tin sleep eyes. Bubbles was modeled after an adorable real baby, and she even cries when turned over. Although her lace-trimmed organdy dress and bonnet are not her original clothes, they are authentically copied from the outfit originally worn by Bubbles many years ago. Beneath her dress was a lace-trimmed combination suit and petticoat, white half socks, and soft leather baby shoes. EFFanBEE dolls were known as "the dolls with the golden hearts," since nearly all of them wore a gold chain with a gold heart, either around their necks or as a wrist bracelet.

While waiting to be picked up and loved, she sits in a child-size wicker rocker that also was made during the 1920s. Perhaps a little boy once sat and rocked his Teddy Bear in this rocker on the wide front porch of a comfortable, white frame house, with a spindle rail running along the length of the porch.

With little stretch of the imagination, we can see the little boy soon becoming restless and running out into the moonlit yard to catch "lightning bugs" (or "fireflies"), which he would trap in a glass jar and hide beneath the pillow of his bed. When he was presumed to be asleep, he would sneak the jar out and watch the fireflies glow in the dark of his room.

At one end of the big front porch, we would likely see a little girl sitting in an old-fashioned wicker porch swing (painted white, with colorful printed cretonne cushions), singing lullabies to her dolly. The swing was always suspended from the porch ceiling by heavy chains secured to awesome-looking, big metal hooks. With just a little persuasion from the evening breeze, the swing would sway gently, but each stride of the swing would be accompanied by a monotonous, "sing-song," almost hypnotizing groan. Children occupying the swing were not usually content with motion provided by the breeze alone, so its gliding would be speeded up considerably by "foot power." This caused the adults to glance warily towards the ceiling, fearing that a chain may at any moment depart from its hook, jolting its rider to the hard, wood floor of the porch. It did indeed happen many, many times!

Gathered around Bubbles on the oak swing are her playmates, who are about the same age, having been made in the early 1920s. Sitting with their hands touching, as if to break into a spell of the "giggles" at any given moment, are five dolls which were very popular with little girls at this time. The first doll on the left is Betsy, a plain old "Ma-Ma" doll with composition head, arms, and legs, on a cloth body stuffed with sawdust or horsehair, with blue tin eyes that open and close. When she was new, she had a "squawker" in her tummy that cried "Ma-Ma" when she was tipped forward. That part of her anatomy has been out of order for at least 50 years. Her face is lined with many cracks and her mohair wig, which once was a dancing mass of curls, now is frazzled and fuzzy. She is dressed in a green cotton romper dress with panties attached, and the pocket has an embroidered flowerpot design. With

Photo 18: On the front porch, in the wicker rocker are "Bubbles," a 25-inch doll made by EFFanBEE, and, in the swing (left to right), Betsy, "Sweety Pie," Betty Lou, Dorie, and Mary Jane, a group of baby dolls. When new, all but "Sweety Pie" cried "Ma-Ma."

it, she wears a quaint, old, cotton print sunbonnet on her head. Her patent leather slippers button at the instep, but they are so old they are split at the front, allowing her big toe to come poking through the end of the shoe. These are strong indications that Betsy was once a much-loved, much-played-with doll, sometime around 1922.

Not a "Ma-Ma" doll, but from a little later period than Bubbles, is another popular doll made by EFFanBEE, called "Sweetie Pie," made around the late 1930s and early 1940s. Sweetie Pie, sitting beside Betsy, has a composition head with jointed composition body. Her legs are bent so she can either lie flat or sit up straight. She has a rooted wig of curly lamb's wool, and brown, tin sleep eyes and eyelashes. She is dressed in a six-month size, yellow Philippine baby dress with yellow crocheted cap, yellow petticoat, panties, and booties.

Betty Lou, in the center of the swing, was a favorite old "Ma-Ma" doll, made around 1920, by Ideal Doll Company. She has a composition head, arms, and legs, and a "huggable" cloth body. At the back of her neck, she has wrinkles or fat creases just as an infant would. She has blue sleep eyes of tin, with molded brown hair, and a tiny rosebud mouth. Insider her tummy is a mechanical device which causes her to cry "Ma-Ma" when she is turned over on your lap. She is dressed in a diaper, long petticoat, long white batiste christening dress trimmed in hand-crocheted lace at the hem and sleeves, long white stockings, and blue booties. She wears a crocheted cap edged in blue ribbon.

Next to Betty Lou is Dorie, a 23-inch "Ma-Ma" doll with composition head, arms, and legs, and a firmly stuffed cloth body. She has brown, tin sleep eyes and eyelashes, and she too cried "Ma-Ma" when she was new, around 1928. She is large enough to be dressed in a six-month size infant's dress of white batiste with pink and blue embroidery, and she wears a pink cotton pique bonnet and pink wool baby booties.

The doll on the far right is Mary Jane, another old "Ma-Ma" doll, about the same age as Betsy, but a trifle larger in size. She has similar construction of composition head, original brown mohair wig with "Dutch" bangs, brown sleep eyes of tin, and brown eyelashes. She has composition arms and legs on a cloth body, but her arms move in a socket at the shoulder like the Bubbles doll. Mary Jane is dressed in a pink and white, checked gingham play dress with a large pink hairbow, white socks and black, shiny, patent leather shoes. Both Mary Jane and Betsy are marked "A. © M. Co." on the backs of their necks. This is the mark of the American Character Doll Company, which was in business a full span of fifty years, from 1918 until 1968.

7. Seeing Double

Photo 19: Three sets of twins: Johnny and Josie, in the wicker cradle, are 9-inch "Rockabye Babies" made around 1924; sitting next to them are Janie and Judy, fifteen-inch "Tiny Tears" dolls with lifelike rubber arms and legs, made in the early 1940s; and standing are Hans and Ilse who have composition heads and cloth feet in wooden shoes, made in the 1930s.

Even in the doll world, twins are a reality and just as much a source of pleasure to their "pretend-like" mamas as they are in real life. Presented here are several sets of twins of varying sizes and materials.

Johnny and Josie, in the wicker cradle, are "Rockabye Babies," 9 inches long, manufactured by Armand Marseille around 1924. Both have bisque heads with sleeping blue eyes, fat cheeks, and open mouths with two little teeth. Their socket heads turn on their jointed composition bodies. They are dressed in matching old lace christening dresses with matching lace bonnets, one as a boy, the other as a girl. Johnny's dress and bonnet are trimmed in blue ribbon, and he has a blue knit sweater and cap; Josie's dress and bonnet are trimmed with pink ribbon, and she has a pink knit sweater and cap. Johnny has a tiny, old, blue and white rattle on his lap, and Josie has a nursing bottle.

Janie and Judy, next to Johnny and Josie, are "Tiny Tears" dolls, 15 inches high, manufactured by American Character Doll Company in the early 1940s. Janie is a blonde, and Judy a brunette, identical in size, and both have blue sleep eyes with lashes. They have hard plastic socket heads that turn on jointed bodies of rubber, with rubber arms and legs. Their hands open in a down position. The use of rubber for doll bodies was introduced in the late thirties because of its soft life-like feeling. However, it was soon discovered that rubber is very perishable, and dolls made of this material must be kept at a cool room temperature and not exposed to excessive heat, or their bodies will crack and flake. This pair is dressed "nearly alike" in pink dresses and blue cap and sweater outfits, but one wears blue booties and the other pink leather shoes. These dolls have tear ducts at the corners of their eyes and an open nursing mouth. Feeding Janie and Judy with a small nursing bottle had the interesting effect of causing tears to run down their faces.

The 15-inch tall pair standing at the rear are Hans and Ilse, a Dutch boy and girl, with composition heads and googly eyes, on cloth bodies. Both have wooden shoes on cloth feet. Hans is dressed in red flannel pants, navy felt jacket, and slouch cap; Ilse wears a red print play dress. They were manufactured during the late 1930s, probably in the United States, though they are unmarked. Their composition heads have well-sculpted curly hair.

In the next photo, number *20*, on the far left, are twins made in Japan between 1920 and 1925. Bobby and Robbie are boy and girl twins who stand just 3½ inches tall. They are all bisque, with molded clothes and hair. Both Bobby and Robbie have fat rosy cheeks, blonde hair, and brown eyes, and their backs, as well as their fronts, have the same detailed modeling of clothing and hair. Robbie is dressed in yellow dress with white collar and white hat with blue band, and Bobby is dressed in a little sailor middy-type suit with short pants. Both have molded, short white socks and black one-strap shoes.

Next to Bobby and Robbie are the Happifats. They are all bisque, 4 inches tall. Their clothes are molded bisque, and they are typified by their robust "rounded" structure and single lock of hair down through the middle of their heads. Their eyes are widened, with a very intensive look. Only their arms are movable on an otherwise solid bisque body and head. Happifat girl is costumed in a full pink dress with white collar and cuffs, with a blue sash bow in the back. Happifat boy is costumed in beige trousers with a dark green jacket, with white collar and tie. The maker is unknown, there are no marks on the dolls, but they were made in Germany around 1914, based on drawings by Kate Jordan.

Next to the Happifats are Sylvia and Ginny, 3½ inches high, who are all-bisque, identical, twin bathers. Their pink and blue bathing suits are of molded bisque; they have molded wavy blonde hair and large Kewpie type (sometimes called Betty Boop type) eyes looking to the side. The head and body of each doll are formed from one solid piece, with rubber-strung movable arms which are poised as if to jump into the water at any given time. These were made in Japan in 1924 and sold in the "dime" stores for 5 cents each. This same doll was made in graduating sizes up to 6 inches, and the price rose accordingly to 25 or 50 cents. The larger sizes were not predressed in the bisque, but could be dressed by their owners. The doll and all its clothes could be conveniently stored in an empty cigar box, and was a great favorite with little girls of the 1920s.

The infant twins at the far right are current reproductions in all bisque, made by the Schackman Company. This is Abbie and Annie, 5 inches tall, with jointed body, arms, and legs, and molded locks of hair. They are copies of all-bisque baby dolls that were originally made in Germany around 1920. They are beautifully dressed in smocked and embroidered pink dotted swiss, with pink hair bows and crocheted booties.

Photo 20: All-bisque dolls: (left to right) Bobby and Robbie stand 3½ inches tall; the "Happifats" have movable arms and were based on drawings by Kate Jordan; Sylvia and Ginny have Kewpie-type (or Betty Boop-type) eyes looking to the side, and sold for five cents in the dime stores; and Abbie and Annie are copies of baby dolls originally made in Germany in 1920.

8. "Tin" Toys for Boys

There was an era in the late 1920s and early 30s in which the toy market was invaded by a flood of metal toys, especially ones made from tin-plated sheet steel, and commonly referred to as "tin." These tin-type toys were relatively inexpensive, for the most part, and little boys enjoyed visiting the nearest "five and ten cent store" with whatever money they had been able to earn from doing chores at home, or mowing lawns for other people. There they could stroll around the toy counter many times, with a dime or quarter in hand, trying to decide just which toy they wished to buy, before they would finally cause the clerk to lose her patience with them, whereupon she would urge them to make up their minds!

There were interesting little wagons pulled by animals, farm-type toys such as tractors and plows, carts and wagons, tin soldiers, and, of course, toy automobiles, which were probably the favorite of all. Most metal toys were brightly painted with a baked-on finish. They were well constructed, and some of the later ones even had a motorized mechanism which could be wound up so the toy would move across the floor on its own.

Most little boys would pool their resources of metal toys when they played together, so each could enjoy a bigger variety of playthings. In combining their toys, there was also the added benefit of sharing their imaginative ideas. What one didn't think of, the others did. This is not to say that quarrels did not ensue, as each boy vied for popularity and acceptance of his ideas. But even if they fought, grabbed up their toys and stalked homeward, it would only be a few minutes until the group would again gather on the sidewalk, for it didn't take them long to realize that it was better to cope with disagreement than to have to play by themselves.

Shown in *Photo 21* are a variety of metal toys typical of this era, some inexpensive at that time, others more costly. The large fireman's truck is obviously one of the more expensive of this kind of toy, and probably would have been found only in homes of the more wealthy children of that time. It is 36 inches long, was made around 1920 in the U.S.A., of iron and steel. It is red, to be sure, and when new, water actually spewed from the hose and the long ladder could be cranked to an aerial working height. Many little boys longed to become firemen when they grew up, so this truck was certain to provide plenty of excitement for those who were fortunate enough to own one, and may have influenced some of our present-day firemen to choose that profession.

Lee, the boy doll by the truck, has a metal head made by Minerva Company in 1905. He is 12 inches tall, with molded blonde wavy hair. He has a kidalene (imitation leather) body and legs, with composition hands. He is dressed in a sailor suit with navy-colored sailor beret, with red and white-striped dickey at the neck of the sailor middy. He wears striped knee socks and black shoes.

Photo 21: Lee, in the sailor suit, and "Charlie McCarthy" (Edgar Bergen's famous dummy character), sitting in front of him, are surrounded by an assortment of metal toys, some mechanized, such as the "Charley Weaver" bartender who runs on batteries.

The toy airplane was made around 1915, and was inspired as a World War I wartime toy. It is olive drab in color, with the U.S. insignia of red, white, and blue. It has a metal "pilot" in the cockpit, and has a single engine with one propellor—a very early aviation-type toy.

The little tin car, with two figures (a man and a boy) riding in it, is of a slightly earlier period than the '20s, having been made in Germany around 1912 by Ernst Paul Lehmann. The firm originally made tins and containers, but they began to manufacture brightly lithographed cars and toys, mechanized by a clockwork motor, and they are still in production near Nuremburg, Germany.

During the early 1930s, a vaudeville and radio act became tremendously popular with adults and children alike, when Edgar Bergen created his famous wooden dummy, whom he fondly called "Charlie McCarthy." Bergen was born in 1903 in Chicago. He wanted to be a doctor, but he adopted ventriloquism as a means of financing his pre-med studies. This led to a more lucrative career, and he abandoned the medical career. He played vaudeville until 1936, then Rudy Vallee hired him for his radio show for one year. He later went into television, appearing on all the better shows, including one of his own, and was still popular and active in show business until his death in November 1978. Bergen and Charlie were inseparable, since one was not adequate without the other, and Edgar Bergen was so skilled in ventriloquism that it was virtually impossible to see his lips move when he projected his voice to make it seem as though Charlie was doing the talking. Not only was Bergen talented in "throwing his voice," but he was able to manipulate the mechanical devices within Charlie so smoothly that Charlie's mouth opened and closed at just the right times, and he appeared to be talking and gesturing with his hands. Charlie delighted in poking fun at Edgar every chance he got—it almost seemed as though he was human at times, and he could gain the sympathy of the entire audience just by a few well chosen remarks about Edgar. As a result of this clever pair, the Charlie McCarthy doll sprung up all over the country, and was especially popular with little boys who would not otherwise have been "caught" playing with a doll. Lovable Charlie, with his famous monocle over his right eye, is shown here, driving a black and white metal truck, positioned in front of the big fire engine.

The Charley Weaver bartender toy to the right of Charlie McCarthy, is a combination metal and plastic mechanical toy made around the late 1940s. Charley Weaver was a character conceived by the late Cliff Arquette. Arquette was born in Toledo, Ohio, in 1905, and was a well-known comedian and character actor whose career began in radio in 1936. Even though a young man, he specialized in portraying aging charcters. He was on radio shows for many years, then got into the movies and later television shows. From 1958 until his death in November 1974, he appeared on NBC-TV's Jack Paar Show and other TV programs, as Charley Weaver, "a wild old man." Charley always had his hat rolled up in front, and dressed like a "country bumpkin." The doll portion of this toy is soft vinyl, and he is dressed in shirt, tie, trousers and suspenders, with his usual flat felt hat. He holds a funnel in one hand, and a measuring cup in the other. His bar is made of brightly painted metal, and when functioning as a battery-operated toy, Charley was animated so that he would raise his right hand and pour "liquid" from the measuring cup through the funnel into a glass on the bar.

The "Magic Lantern," at far right in the picture, is one of the earliest ones of its kind and possibly had a direct effect on what was about to happen in the entertainment world, with the early moving pictures which were gaining in popularity and creativity. This toy originally was marketed with glass slides having several frames of the cartoon type which a child could push through the projector and show on a wall. It was made in the U.S.A. around 1890. It is thought that the reason for the stove pipe on its top was because it had an oil burner inside, which provided the light needed to project the slides. Some were later electrified.

9. "Tin" Toys for Girls

While there was not a great variety of tin-type or metal toys made for girls, there were, nevertheless, some very *significant* metal dolls and toys made for girls.

Metal doll heads had been made as early as 1861, but they were not produced in great quantity until about 1919 to 1923. There seemed to be a need for what could be considered an "unbreakable" doll during this period, so metal doll heads became very important, and several kinds of metal dolls were manufactured for that purpose. Some were made of sheet brass, some were sheet metal, others were made from either lead, copper, zinc, aluminum, or tin, but nearly all were coated with a washable flesh-colored enamel, with painted features and hair. One of the better-known tin-type dolls was made by Minerva Manufacturing Company prior to 1900, and another was the Juno doll head made in 1904 by Karl Standfuss and distributed by George Borgfeldt Company. The doll heads had attractively painted faces and painted wavy hair. In most cases, the metal head was put on a cloth body, with either cloth or leather arms and legs. Because they were thought to be unbreakable, children were inclined to be more abusive in handling them; consequently, most old metal dolls have chipped places on their noses and cheeks, where they fell to the sidewalk or were otherwise badly treated.

Shown in *Photo 22* is a group of "tin head" dolls. Number 1 on the left is 9-inch tall Charline, made in the U.S.A. around 1915. She is a laughing baby with metal head on a cardboard stump base, instead of legs. When her stomach is pressed, she says "Ma-Ma." She is dressed in an old pink cotton dress and matching bonnet.

Another popular toy, which was made of chrome-plated steel and wood, is the toy telephone shown here. Every little girl adored her toy telephone and enjoyed pretending to make important conversations over the phone—one of the most fun things to do when playing "House." Many little girls would pretend to call the grocery store and place an order for groceries to be delivered, or they would call their friends and exchange small talk, but perhaps the most fun of all was pretending that a boyfriend was calling, and a romantic conversation would develop. The base and mouthpiece of the telephone were made of metal, and the receiver was wood. At the back of the telephone, there was a device which, when jiggled with the finger, would make a jingling sound like the ring of a telephone. This was always the first part of the toy phone to wear out or need repair, because of frequent usage.

The doll with her hand holding the telephone receiver is Jasmine, 19 inches tall, with a bisque head on a ball-jointed composition body. She is dressed in pink dotted Swiss, with a pink hair ribbon on her blonde wig, and she has strikingly beautiful blue eyes. Jasmine was made about 1915. Her head is marked "109-11," and

Photo 22: Tin-head dolls: (clockwise from left) Caroline, who cries "Ma-Ma" when her tummy is pressed; Jasmine, with a bisque head, holds a tin telephone; Vicky; Harriett; Bernice; and Lucy, with red hair.

she is possibly an unmarked Kestner. Her body was made by Handwerck.

Number 3 (second from left, back row) is Vicky, a 13-inch metal head from 1925, an unmarked doll on a cloth body, with composition hands. She is dressed in an olive green coat and has a bow in her hair. She is a Patsy-type redhead with brightly painted hair. Since nearly every doll manufacturer tried to copy EFFanBEE's Patsy doll, this could possibly have been the metal head look-alike for Patsy.

Number 4 (far right, back row) is Harriett, a 15-inch metal head by Minerva Company (made around 1910) on a pink cloth body with composition arms. She is in excellent condition with good painted features and blonde wavy hair. She is dressed in a grey striped cotton dress with white and black star-printed apron.

Number 5 (front row, middle) is Lucy, a 13-inch unmarked baby doll with metal head on a cloth body, and composition hands. She was probably made around 1924. She has painted red hair, sleeping blue eyes, and is dressed in a pink baby dress trimmed with blue ribbons. On her lap is an old metal wind-up toy duck.

Number 6 (far right, front row) is Bernice, a 12-inch metal head by Minerva Company, made around 1900, with a pink cloth body and composition arms. She is dressed in a white cotton material with pink rose print, and it is nicely trimmed in tiny buttons and lace ruffles.

10. Tin Soldiers

A complete battle scene is reenacted here in *Photo 23* through this group of 64 metal soldiers, none of which is over 3 inches tall, and each characterized by varying duties and types of fire arms or radio equipment. The uniforms and metal hats are reminiscent of those worn by the fighting men during World War I, with their khaki-color uniforms, leg wraps, and high leather boots. This toy must have been produced during the period 1914-1918.

At the left of the picture is the marching band, represented by three drummers, fife players, coronet players, a drum major, and a color bearer. Toward the back of the band is a medical unit, complete with a wounded soldier on a stretcher, being carried by two litter bearers, two doctors and a nurse in white uniforms, another doctor in khaki uniform, with medical kit in hand, plus two "walking wounded" on crutches.

At center back, inside the headquarters tent, is the adjutant sitting at a wooden table with typewriter in front of him. The adjutant was like an office clerk, who kept the company records and helped to administer the orders of the commanding officer. Scattered throughout the picture at right are many infantrymen with guns at various angles, two soldiers with gas masks on, some with binoculars spotting the enemy far away, others relaying the information to headquarters via their radio equipment, and still others who would fire the big cannons boldly positioned towards the front line. The row of white trench bags symbolizes the many bags of sand, which in war-torn areas, would be stacked above a dug trench to act as a barrier behind which the soldiers could hide while waiting their chances to shoot at the enemy.

Toward the center front is a single soldier leading a German Shepherd dog, which was useful in detecting the presence of poison gases. One of the most unique of all are the two soldiers just below the flagpole who are preparing to release the carrier pigeons, which in some isolated areas provided the only means of getting messages back and forth between units.

It is regrettable that war has always been a tragic reality in history, and it is not easy to understand how children can actually enjoy playing with toy soldiers, but nonetheless, this was a very popular and exciting toy.

Photo 23: A battle scene is reenacted here with 64 metal soldiers, none over 3 inches tall.

11. 'Lectric Train

One of the favorite toys for boys, from about 1920 on, was the electric train. Our country was still largely dependent upon trains for travel at that time, so toy trains were a very important symbol of the times and reflected the destiny of many little boys who dreamed of being engineers when they grew up. Little boys and their fathers would spend hours on their hands and knees, playing train conductors and engineers, and often became so deeply involved in railroading that the call to come to the table for dinner went almost unheeded.

Almost synonymous with electric trains is the name *Lionel.* When he was seven years old, Joshua Lionel Cowen designed a tiny steam engine and placed it in a hand-carved wooden locomotive. By the time he was nineteen, he had developed a tiny electric motor and decided to manufacture electric trains—giving the company his middle name. His early creations were simple models of trolleys and electrics. The appeal of the trains was immediate, but sales were restricted by limited manufacturing capabilities and the fact that few homes had electricity in 1900. Cowen's main customers were stores, who used the trains for window displays. But as the use of electricity increased, so did sales, and in 1910 *Lionel* began to mass produce. In 1915 it expanded its line to include trains that ran on O-gauge, three-rail track. The older trains had run on wider track, called "standard" gauge, also three-rail, which Cowen had developed. By the middle 1920s, *Lionel* began making models of steamers. Some of these old trains were huge, standing as high as a child's knee and stretching eight feet along the track.

Cowen was aware of the popularity of the diesel engines, but never became a fan of them. He preferred the action of the driving rods on steam engines.

"Richard," who is sitting by the train in *Photo 24*, is a 15-inch tall Kestner boy doll manufactured in 1915. He has a bisque head with intense blue eyes, and a human hair wig of auburn, with a toddler jointed composition body. He is dressed in blue and white checked wool jacket and knickers, socks, and shoes.

"Jimmy," the engineer, is a Buddy Lee boy doll, 13 inches tall, of composition one-piece body and head with moving arms, and was made in 1945. He has molded painted hair, with painted black eyes, side glancing, and painted black boots. He is dressed in denim cap and overalls with breast pocket which holds a tiny pencil and railroad time record. These clothes were made by Kay Johnson and are an excellent, precise copy of the overalls and cap originally made by H. D. Lee Company for their trademark doll. He is marked "Buddy Lee" on the back. Richard and Jimmy are fascinated by the chug-chug of the train as it moves over the miniature railroad track, through the tunnel, and over the bridge. The metal tunnel and bridge are from the early 1940s.

The train is all metal, with a black steam engine, authentically painted connecting flat cars and red caboose, manufactured in 1941, just prior to World War II. When one pulled the lever of the little black transformer, the engine would lurch forward on the metal train track and pull its shiny caravan of cars behind it, but its inevitable downfall was always the fact that the train engine moved at such a fast clip that it usually ended in derailment. But then, that was where little boy engineers became important; they would rush to the scene of the accident and patiently recouple the engine and all cars, and put them back on course for another fast-moving trip around the oval track.

Photo 24: Jimmy, the engineer, is a 13-inch Buddy Lee doll made in 1945; Richard is a 15-inch Kestner boy made in 1915; and the train set dates from 1941.

Some of the more elaborate train sets had lots of extra metal track pieces which would even produce a figure-8 track, and some little black engines had tiny flashlight size bulbs in their headlights, which would cast a beam of light down the track ahead of them.

12. Big Boys' Trains

Just as women never get too old to collect and enjoy dolls, so it is with grown men and boys who have a love for miniature trains. The design and production of the scale models followed on the heels of the toy trains and this hobby has never stopped being a very popular pastime for men ever since.

During the 1940s and 1950s, Joshua Lionel Cowen became increasingly interested in action-oriented cars and accessories. On the *Lionel* line, little toy men unloaded milk cans from "reefers," cattle scooted on and off the cattle cars, logs got sawed in lumber mills, and coal stations poured coal into hoppers. Lights blinked on crossing signals, twirled on searchlight cars, and rotated on towers.

Lionel's closest competitor was the *American Flyer* trains, which were made in Chicago. One thing Cowen did not foresee was the growth of scale model trains, both larger and smaller than the ones *Lionel* made, and their introduction into the *Lionel* market. Sales began to falter, and by 1958 Cowen had retired. In 1959 he put his stock up for sale, and he died in 1965 at the age of 85. *General Mills* purchased Lionel's tooling and leased the name *Lionel* in 1968—the Lionel trains are now made in Mount Clemens, Michigan.

One reason that *General Mills* was interested in *Lionel* was because they realized that the postwar babies of the '40s and '50s were having babies of their own, and they were coming into train-playing age. The parents fondly remembered *Lionel* red and silver diesels and engines that smoked, and they wanted the same for their kids. In 1980 a special train was produced to commemorate the one-hundredth birthday of Joshua Lionel Cowen.

Starting with a basic track layout, an engine, and a few cars is just the beginning to whet the appetite of America's armchair engineers. Each car and each engine is a true miniature, a fraction of the size of regular toy trains which, for so many years, passed over the rails wih their clickety clak rhythmical sounds. There is always something more that can be added to the authenticity of the equipment, the scenery, and the highly efficient mechanism which sends the train around its circuit. Miniature train buffs are not standing still. They are constantly on the lookout for a different item to enhance their existing scenes. Likewise, the manufacturers of scale-model equipment are constantly upgrading their products to satisfy the whims of these collectors.

Photos 25 and *26* show a prime example of the never-ending fun and challenge of one of the most popular model train sizes, called HO gauge. To look at this complicated intertwining layout of tracks, trees, storefronts, and the like, we might conclude that the owner of this handsome layout could not find room for one more thing. However, this would come as a great disappointment to him if indeed he could not continue to search for "one more locomotive or

Photo 25 & 26: Here (and in the next photo) is an intricate layout of a modern HO gauge train set.

Photo 27: This model locomotive won an award for its flawless paint job.

flatcar," for that is the purest form of excitement: the anticipation of another one to be found and placed in just the right spot in the scene.

A sideline to this hobby is the tasteful art of repainting cars by experts in this field, which involves tedious, time-consuming effort to make the cars appear older than they look right after being freshly painted. This necessitates giving them a coat of special paint, which leaves the illusion of smoke or dust covering the otherwise bright and shiny new paint. *Photo 27* shows just such a locomotive which has earned its owner an award for its flawless paint job.

13. Kewpie Cuties

Rose O'Neill Wilson was born in Pennsylvania in 1874, but spent most of her life in Missouri. While in her early thirties, she created a doll which immediately became very popular, and still is, to this day. Her fat-tummied cherubic Kewpie doll first appeared merely as an angel head in *Puck* magazine. Soon after that, she began to draw the complete Kewpie figure, accompanied by her own verses. This full page of winsome illustrations and words appeared first in *Ladies' Home Journal* in 1909, then later appeared as paper dolls with clothes in *Woman's Home Companion* and *Good Housekeeping* magazines. *Photo 28* has as its background a page entitled "The Kewpies and the Little German Girl" as it appeared in the August 1913 issue of *Woman's Home Companion.* Magazines were at that time much larger in dimension than they now are, this sheet being 11 by 16 inches.

The delightful Kewpie image took America by storm, and Rose O'Neill soon presented an actual doll to the world, in the form of an all-bisque Kewpie which was patented in 1913. These early Kewpies were made both in bisque and in celluloid in Germany by J. D. Kestner and distributed by George Borgfeldt & Company of New York. Later they were made with composition heads and cloth bodies, as well as rubber and wood. They were largely made with legs together, with outstretched arms and starfish hands, and eyes glancing either to the right or left. However, Rose O'Neill soon modified this style to include many clever characters, such as "Wag, the Chief," "The Army," "The Cook," "The Gardener," and many other adorable creations, including one of her most famous, two Kewpies with arms around each other, known as "The Huggers."

In subsequent years, the Kewpie likeness appeared on hundreds of novelty items such as soap, dishes, ceramic boxes, and so on.

In *Photo 28*, the 13-inch-tall composition jointed Kewpie was made between 1916 and 1941. Joseph Kallus, president of Cameo Doll Company, worked with Rose O'Neill and was responsible for the production of all wood pulp (composition) Kewpies such as this one. These were distributed by the George Borgfeldt Company.

The large composition Kewpie is surrounded by a group of eleven all-bisque Kewpies in varying sizes and poses, but characteristic of all of them are their happy little watermelon-shaped mouths, the top-knot of painted hair, and the little blue wings on the shoulders. Some still have the famous heart-shaped sticker on the chest which was the Kewpie trademark, if designed by Rose O'Neill. These were all made in Germany between 1913 and 1926. Some of the more familiar ones in this picture are "The Traveler," with his suitcase in one hand and umbrella in the other; "The Lawyers" with a book in their hands, and one behind them;

Photo 28: Kewpie dolls first appeared in 1913. Here, the 13-inch composition Kewpie is joined by smaller, all-bisque Kewpies in various poses.

"The Army," with his soldier hat and gun at his side; and "The Huggers" with their arms around one another. The tallest Kewpie is the 8-inch one at left. "The Thinker," 5 inches high, sits with hands under his chin. It is hollow at the bottom, but is marked on the back "Rose O'Neill, Kewpie, Germany." A very unusual one is the pensive one seated in the bisque wicker chair, with arms folded and feet crossed. The side-glancing adorable eyes on these cherubic faces are probably the most notable feature about them, which makes everyone love them as much today as they did when they were first created by the talented Rose O'Neill.

14. Modern Dolls

Photo 29: Modern collectible dolls made between 1950 and 1962: (back row, from left) *Mary Lou, made by Uneeda, "Charmin' Chatty" by Mattel, and "Saucy Walker" by Ideal;* (middle row) *"Honey" by EFFanBEE:* (front row, from left) *Tootsie, an all-vinyl Kewpie, "Tammy" by Ideal, and Olga, made in Italy by Furga.*

This is a group of modern dolls, not antique, but collectible, covering an era between 1950 and 1962. The tallest doll at the back is 25-inch Charmin' Chatty, made in 1961 by Mattel, and a very popular doll at the time. She holds in her hand one of the four records that came with her, and which will still play. By inserting a record in the opening in back of the doll, and pulling the cord, the listener hears an utterance somewhat of the tone quality of Donald Duck, but can nevertheless distinguish the phrases "Happy Birthday," "I want my Mama," or "Hello, my name is Chatty!" She is dressed in her original outfit of sailor middy and skirt, with vinyl saddle shoes.

To the right of Chatty is Saucy Walker, 22 inches tall, made by Ideal Doll Company in 1951. She is all hard plastic, with plump legs and arms, flirty eyes and lashes, and with long brown hair which can be braided; one can make her walk along, turning her head as she walks. She is dressed, not in her original outfit, but in a white blouse and plaid flared skirt with straps over the shoulders, white socks, and black leather shoes.

At left rear is Mary Lou, a 22-inch doll made by *Uneeda* Company, around 1950, with soft vinyl head on a hard plastic body, blue sleep eyes, and blonde rooted hair. She is dressed in peach-colored pajamas. Uneeda Company began making dolls in 1917, and they are still in operation.

At left in front of Mary Lou is Honey, 16 inches tall, with durable hard plastic head, sleeping blue eyes, and blonde rooted Saran hair, on a slim, jointed plastic body, manufactured by EFFanBEE around 1952. She is dressed in green and white dotted pajamas, and a green corduroy bathrobe with heart-shaped pockets, and red felt boots.

In front of Charmin' Chatty is Tammy, a 12-inch plastic doll with slender body, jointed straight legs and arms, and made in 1962 by Ideal Doll Company. She has blue sleep eyes and rooted, blonde Saran hair. She is not in her original outfit, but is dressed like a high school girl in plaid skirt, blouse, and yellow knit sweater. With it, she wears long nylon stockings and low-heeled loafers.

To the right of Tammy is Olga, 13 inches tall, an all-vinyl doll made in Italy around 1961 by Furga. Their dolls always have pretty eyes and long lashes, and an abundance of lovely, long, rooted hair. This one is dressed in a short cotton dress with green vinyl coat with fake fur sleeves, boots to match, and imitation white fur cossack hat.

At far left is Tootsie, a modern vinyl Kewpie, 10 inches tall and made by Cameo Doll Company (design by Joseph Kallus) in 1962. She is made entirely of vinyl with a one-piece body. Her arms and legs are in a stationary position, but her head turns, and she has stationary, blue, glass eyes glancing to the side. One foot has the signature of Rose O'Neill on the bottom, and the other is marked Kewpie. She is dressed in a typical Kewpie-style sunsuit. Joseph Kallus originally owned the Cameo Company, which was founded in 1922 and which was sold in 1970 to Strombecker Corporation. The vinyl Kewpies are being produced from original molds by Rose O'Neill.

15. Antique & Modern, Black & White

Photo 30: Antique and modern, black and white: (left to right) "Patsy," made in 1925; Peaches, made in 1967; Susie Jane, made in Japan around 1915, whose crib companion is a reproduction of the Grace Storey Putnam Byelo *baby; Charlotte, made in 1910; Cindy, made in Germany in 1910; "So-Wee Sunbabe," made in 1956; and "Amosandra," a "drink and wet" dolly made in the 1930s.*

Patsy and "Peaches," at far left in *Photo 30,* are playmates, both 14 inches tall. Patsy is an all-composition doll with swivel head, small painted mouth, painted eyes looking to the side, molded and painted straight bobbed auburn hair, and a painted hair ribbon over her bangs. She has slender straight legs, jointed at the hips; and a characteristic of all Patsy dolls was the outstretched left arm, the right arm bent at the elbow.

Patsy was introduced in 1925 by the EFFanBEE Company. She was first manufactured in 1924 with a stuffed cloth body and limbs, and a stationary head of composition. However, the most popular version of Patsy was the all-composition one first placed on the market in 1927. Patsy is dressed in a light-green cotton pique dress trimmed in lace, with a perky matching off-the-face hat.

There followed a family of Patsy dolls, as EFFanBEE created the Patsy, Jr., Patsy-Ann, Patsy-Joan, Patsy Lou, Patsy Ruth, Patsy Mae, Wee Patsy, and Patsyette, plus others, all with similar faces and expressions, though varying in size from 5 inches to 29 inches tall. The Patsy family was extremely popular, and continued to be made from 1927 until World War II. Production of Patsy resumed

Photo 31: (left to right) Eunice is 18 inches tall with a papier mache body and wooden arms; Hattie Mae was made by puppeteer Tony Sarg in the 1940s; Aunt Het has a papier mache head, made in Germany around 1900; "Tickletoes" was made in 1927 and sold by Sears Roebuck; "Tickletoes" holds Bess, a black composition doll made around 1930; Florence, made in 1915, has "flirty" eyes which roll to the side; and Mabel has an unusual bisque head with a closed mouth.

again from 1946 until 1950. Wigs and sleep eyes were added after 1932, but the most admired and sought after Patsy remains the one pictured here.

"Peaches" is an adorable black vinyl doll with black curly hair and brown glass eyes, made by the Horsman Doll Company in 1967. She is dressed in a peach-colored organdy ruffled "Sunday School" dress, with a matching hat, both trimmed in lace.

At far right, in the wicker basket is Amosandra, a 10-inch tall, all-rubber black baby doll with jointed arms and legs, brown molded hair, and molded and painted brown eyes and features. She is a "drink and wet" dolly, having a hole in her lips where she can be given water from a tiny nursing bottle, and a small opening at the back where she can be counted on to wet her diaper. Amosandra was manufactured by the Sun Rubber Company of Barberton, Ohio, and patented by the *Columbia Broadcasting System*, who sponsored the radio program called "Amos and Andy," back in the 1930s, to portray Amos and Ruby's baby in that show.

The white baby, also 10 inches tall, is named "So-Wee Sunbabe," a vinyl, jointed doll also made by Sun Rubber Company, and created by Ruth E. Newton in 1956. He has stationary, blue, glass eyes, molded light-brown hair, and an open nursing mouth, and is also a "drink and wet" doll.

The tall doll in the center of the photograph is Charlotte, an outstanding black doll whose story appears in the chapter, *A Pretty Girl.*"

In the little white baby crib at left is Susie Jane, a 4-inch tall, black painted, all-bisque, jointed, baby doll with black hair tufts tied in red ribbons and dressed in tiny, red and white polka dot dress. She was made in Japan around 1915. Her crib companion is a 4-inch all-bisque jointed reproduction of the Grace Storey Putnam Byelo baby made by Mabel Oliphant. She is dressed in a peach-colored knit pram suit and cap.

At the right rear is Cindy, a 14-inch tall, black doll with bisque head and jointed composition body and was made in Germany in 1910. Her black wool hair is in tiny braids tied with red ribbons. She is dressed in a cotton print dress of white with blue dots with a blue belt at the low waistline. She is marked "Germany 503/0."

In *Photo 31*, at far left is Eunice, an 18-inch-tall doll with bisque head on ball-jointed body of papier mache and wooden arms and legs, and was made by C. M. Bergmann in 1916. She has blue, sleep eyes and blonde eyelashes and wig of long curls. She is dressed in a blue and yellow printed voile dress with low waistline with sash that ties in a big bow in the back. She wears her original mesh stockings and white party shoes, and black velvet bonnet.

Next to Eunice is Hattie Mae, a 17-inch tall, black doll of composition head, arms, and legs, and a cloth body; she was made by puppeteer Tony Sarg in the early 1940s. It is thought that she was expressly designed for sale at the Kentucky Derby. She has all her original clothes—a red and white dotted cotton dress covered with a crisp white organdy apron, and a red bandana around her head.

Behind Hattie Mae is Aunt Het, an unmarked 26-inch, black doll made in Germany around 1900. Her head is of papier mache with a laughing open/closed mouth, glass eyes, and a cloth body. She wears a faded blue polka dot cotton housedress with red checked gingham apron.

To the right of Aunt Het is Florence, an 18-inch tall doll with bisque head and the original mohair wig. She has pierced ears, and a ball-jointed composition body, and was made in 1915 by Simon & Halbig and Kammer & Reinhardt. She has "flirty" eyes, meaning that her eyes are specially made to roll to the side instead of looking only straight ahead. Simon & Halbig was a porcelain factory in Germany that made bisque, celluloid, and composition dolls' heads as early as 1870 and as late as the 1920s. Kammer & Reinhardt was a partnership equally as important to the doll industry, and responsible for many improvements in doll eyes. In later years, Simon & Halbig made many of the bisque heads for Kammer & Reinhardt, hence the combination of names as shown here. Florence is attractively dressed in a pink cotton dress with gathered skirt and lace Bertha collar and trim.

At far right is Mabel, an 18-inch tall doll made in Germany, unmarked except for the "No. 206" and "Germany." She has an unusual bisque head with closed mouth, on a jointed composition body, and curly blonde wig with blue hair ribbon. She is dressed in a fashionable beige silk with pleated skirt edged with brown satin ribbon. The top of the dress has a brown shirred inset bodice with seven little pearl buttons down the front. She has mesh stockings and brown leather boots with tassels at the top.

In the foreground, directly behind the orange blossoms, is an 18-inch tall baby doll called "Tickletoes" made in 1927 and sold by *Sears Roebuck.* She has a composition head with flirty eyes, dimples in her cheeks, molded and painted blonde baby hair, rubber arms and legs, and a cloth body. She has on her original outfit of light blue organdy infant dress and bonnet with large ruffle framing her face, and her original tag which says, "Tickletoes—I have rubber arms and legs—squeeze my leg and I cry."

Tickletoes is holding Bess, an adorable black baby doll made in the U.S.A. around 1930. Bess is 12 inches long, with composition head and painted facial features, with jointed composition body. She is dressed in a white and blue printed romper suit, and her black braids are tied with red ribbons.

At the beginning of the 1940s, manufacture of composition dolls was rapidly being replaced by newer materials such as plastics and vinyls. Vinyl has even replaced hard plastic in most cases, because of its durability in any kind of weather. It does not crack, craze, or turn brown when exposed to extreme heat or cold.

Ideal Doll Company developed a new type of synthetic rubber which looked and felt like human skin, and called it Magic Skin. It seemed like the perfect answer to a life-like soft babyish body, but eventually it became obvious that it was even more fragile than rubber, and after a time the "skin" often turned brown and became flaky, especially if it were not stored at an even temperature. If exposed to high temperatures, the "Magic Skin" turned dark brown.

In *Photo 32* we see an interesting contrast between the old and the new. Rosie, at left, is a 15-inch baby doll made in 1941 by Arranbee Doll Company, another American doll manufacturer. She has a hard plastic head, but her body is made of Magic Skin. This one has been well cared for, is in excellent condition, almost like new, with molded painted hair, blue sleeping eyes, and is dressed in a pink cotton baby dress with white collar, pearl buttons, and two pockets with lace and embroidery trim. She wears a pink knit baby bonnet and booties.

Jeannette, the other baby doll in this bassinette, is a 16-inch-tall character baby made in Germany by Kammer & Reinhardt. She is marked K ✡ R No. 126," Simon & Halbig. She has a bisque head on a bent-leg, jointed composition body. Her brown eyes not only close like a sleeping baby, but they will also remain open when the doll is laid down, closing only when the doll is turned on its side. She has an open mouth with two teeth, and wears a diaper, slip, and old, white, dimity baby dress with lace insertions and pink ribbon beading, with a frilly, white, smocked bonnet, and knit booties.

Blending the generation gap between the old and the new is an old crib toy molded with a baby riding on Mother Goose's back. It was made around 1925, of rubber, in pastel colors of blue, pink, and white.

Photo 32: Rosie, a fifteen-inch baby doll made in 1941 (with a body made of ''Magic Skin'' which is remarkably similar to human skin), is contrasted with Jeannette, made in 1920 with a composition body and bisque head. Between them is a rubber crib toy made around 1925.

Photo 33: The tallest of this group is 9-inch Doris, made in 1910; in front of her is "Wendy Ann," made in 1956; and in the lace cap is "Little Genius," made by Madame Alexander in 1957. The other dolls, all celluloid were made during the 1920s.

Photo 34: (Left to right) *"Ginnette" is an infant doll introduced in 1956 (part of the Ginny series by Vogue Doll Company); Beverly is a Ginny doll from 1948; and "Our Daisy" was made around 1905.*

Photo 33 is a study in antique and modern small dolls—the tallest of this group is Doris, 9 inches with bisque head and stationary blue eyes, on an oatmeal (composition) body. Her wig is not the original, but a pretty blonde mohair with soft ringlets made by Vera Weimer. She is dressed in her original clothes, consisting of silk pongee dress, pale pink ribbon and ecru lace, three cotton petticoats edged in lace, panties, and cotton stockings. Her colonial shoes are all original, of black leather with buckle trim. Her hat is a new addition to the outfit. She is unmarked except for the numbers "1000 10/0," and she was made in Germany around 1910.

In front of Doris is Wendy Ann, an 8-inch tall ballerina, made in the U.S.A. in 1956 by Madame Alexander. (*See* the chapter-*Madame Alexander* for further information on this famous doll maker). Wendy Ann is an all-vinyl doll with jointed knees and elbows, and dark rooted hair. Her pink satin and tulle ballerina costume still bears the Madame Alexander label in the back.

Another small doll made by Madame Alexander is Little Genius, also 8-inches-tall, made in 1957 of vinyl with hard plastic head. She has on her original outfit of blue organdy dress trimmed in lace and pink flowerettes, with a sweet little lace cap. She has a blonde caracul wig which was glued to the head.

The remaining three dolls are all celluloid from the 1920s. The two at left are bent-leg on celluloid bodies. One is an 8-inch-tall baby boy, marked "Royal—Made in Japan." The other is a girl 6 inches tall, with molded blonde hair and pink hair ribbon, made in 1920 and marked "Yanoca—Made in U.S.A."

The older celluloid boy doll has a shoulder head of celluloid marked "American" over a sketch of an Indian head. It has painted molded features and is on a stuffed cloth body. He is dressed in a checked navy gingham suit with wide white collar.

Celluloid dolls were made as early as 1863 in England. The most famous maker of celluloids was Rheinische Gummi & Celluloid Fabrik Company of Bavaria, founded in 1873. They were also made by Cuno and Otto Dressel, Kammer & Reinhardt, and Kestner, in Germany.

In *Photo 34* the winsome looking little plastic doll with bathrobe about to fall off, and tousled blonde wig, is Beverly, an 8-inch tall Ginny doll made in 1950. Ginny dolls were first made in 1947 and continued to be produced for nearly twenty years.

The two dolls at the back are significant for having their original boxes. At left is Ginnette, an 8-inch tall baby doll made by *Vogue* Doll Company. This was the infant doll of the Ginny series, introduced in 1956, and the price on the box at that time was $3.00. At right is an old doll called "Our Daisy"; she is 7½ inches tall, all bisque, with molded painted shoes and socks with blue band, original blonde mohair wig, and brown sleep eyes. She was made around 1905 in Germany. She was not a dressed doll originally, having only white slip and panties when new. She is now nicely dressed in a white silk dress and straw hat, with lace and ribbon trim.

JoAnne, in *Photo 35*, is an unmarked 13-inch all-composition toddler, with jointed arms and legs. She has reddish brown molded hair, with an open mouth and two teeth, and brown sleep eyes with eyelashes. She resembles the Dionne quintuplet dolls, and was made around 1936. She has been beautifully redressed in pink checked organdy, trimmed with tiny lace, and with smocking and embroidered flowers across the yoke of the dress, with a dainty pink organdy slip and her original rayon panties. Her matching pink organdy bonnet is also smocked and embroidered with a tiny pink rose at the crown.

Baby Sue is a darling 5½-inch infant doll of bisque-like composition, made in 1976 by Haudrey. She is fully jointed, and her neck opening has been carefully lined with felt. She has neatly painted features and looks much like a Byelo baby reproduction. The toy scale on which she lies is pink lithographed tin, called "Pla-Scale." It was made in the U.S.A., probably around 1936, and it will actually weigh objects up to two pounds.

Eloise, riding in the red wooden sleigh, is a 6-inch tall, lovely little all-bisque doll, unmarked, but undoubtedly made by J. D. Kestner before 1890. She is made from high-quality smooth bisque, with stationary, blue, glass eyes, well painted features, and with the typical Kestner molded and painted blue-ribbed stockings and brown party slippers. Her mohair wig is new, but her clothes are original, of old batiste panties, petticoat and lace-trimmed dress. Her bonnet is of old crocheted lace.

Georgie is a most unusual mechanical doll, 9 inches tall, with a bisque head made by Heubach, probably around 1900. The facial features are beautifully painted, with a smiling open-closed mouth with two little teeth. The head is marked with the Heubach sunburst mark and the figure "23" written upside down at the back of the neck, plus "Germany" written with the typical Heubach □ . Strangely enough, this doll head appears to be that of a boy,with short molded painted hair, and a definite center crown part. Yet its clothes, all original, are those of a girl. The pink cotton dress is perfectly sized to fit around the robust cylinder body with wheels beneath it, and the hands are of composition on flimsy floppy arms. When wound, the doll glides smoothly across the floor.

Janet is 11 inches high, with a bisque head marked "Germany—80," and she bears a strange mark like this: □ She has a composition jointed body, with unusual painted white stockings, banded in red and black slippers with two straps. She was probably made around 1910. She has stationary brown eyes and an open mouth with four teeth. Her blonde wig is a replacement, and she wears a lovely new party dress of rose printed taffeta, made from old taffeta printed ribbon, with a matching bonnet. Over her arm she carries an old crocheted basket of flowers.

This group of dolls offers still another interesting contrast between the old and the new, as these date from about 1890 to 1976.

Photo 35: (Left to right) *Georgie is an unusual mechanical doll, with bisque head, made by Heubach around 1900; Baby Sue is 5½ inches long, made in 1976, and she is lying on a "Pla-Scale" made around 1936; Jo Anne is an all-composition toddler made around 1936; Eloise, in the wooden sleigh, is a 6-inch-tall, all-bisque doll made around 1890; and Janet is 11 inches tall, made in Germany around 1910.*

16. Cute and Cuddly

As far back as anyone can remember, and even beyond that, cloth dolls and stuffed animals have provided soothing comfort to girls, as well as boys, from infancy through the teens in many cases. Many a child has gone to sleep clutching a soft floppy toy, feeling safer for its companionship and mutual love. Rag dolls date back to the early Egyptians; and up until about 1870, most cloth dolls were handmade by mothers for their children. From about 1880 on, however, many patents were sought as dolls were manufactured and sold commercially by various companies.

Some of the names recognized among these early cloth doll designers were Izannah Walker, Martha Wellington, and perhaps one of the most notable, Martha Chase, who created the famous stockinette doll, shown in *Photo 36* at left, back row. This was called the Chase Play doll, produced from 1891 to 1900, and entirely handmade of woven stockinette. This one is 20 inches long, its head made of stockinette, and the body of pink sateen is stuffed with white cotton batting. The facial features and hair were carefully painted with waterproof paints that were known to be safe for children. This also is indicative of one of the earliest attempts to prevent toys from being injurious to children. After World War II, the Chase factory began making Chase Hospital Dolls in sizes of newborn infant, two-months old, four-months old, one-year old, and four-year old children, plus female and male adult dolls. They were, and still are, widely used by the American Red Cross and in hospitals and home economics classes as educational models of the human body.

The Cuddle Kewpie directly in front of the Chase doll was designed by Rose O'Neill in 1921, and was one of her few attempts at making cloth dolls. This one is 11 inches tall, with typical Kewpie face and side-glancing eyes, and is dressed in a red cotton stuffed suit.

Using the rag doll for advertising purposes became a reality from about 1900 on, and these could often be obtained by saving and mailing a boxtop or side panel from a box of *Cream of Wheat* cereal, *Aunt Jemima* pancake flour, and various other products. Advertising dolls are still being manufactured, collected, and enjoyed by many people.

Another popular concept of cloth dolls were those inspired by comic strips. One of these is Buttercup, to the right of the Chase doll, a 15-inch tall cloth doll with printed design of face and clothes. Buttercup appeared in the old comics called "Toots and Casper" by Jimmy Murphy during the 1920s. On the back of the neck is printed "Copyright 1924 by King Features Syndicate Inc." Buttercup always looked exactly as shown, with one tiny wisp of a curl over the ear, elongated dots for eyes, and with smiling lips.

"Skeezix," the 15-inch tall, lanky, boy doll with one arm over the cradle side, is made of an oilcloth-type fabric and is dressed only in his "birthday suit," except for his brown painted sandals.

Skeezix was the main character in the original "Gasoline Alley" comic strip, around 1924. He was always characterized by the unruly forelock of blonde hair. Cartoonists very often picked a certain feature to exaggerate, which made their creations instantly recognizable.

At left front, with large bunny feet protruding between the cradle posts, is a 20-inch-tall stuffed animal called Uncle Wiggily. This floppy-eared rabbit is a fascinating character created by Howard R. Garis back in the early 1920s. The syndicated column relating his adventures appeared nightly in most newspapers throughout the United States. Numerous books also were published; and even today, one can still buy the game called "Uncle Wiggily."

Uncle Wiggily was affectionately called "the jolly old rabbit gentleman with the pink, twinkling nose," and he did indeed look like a gentleman, for he most often was seen wearing a black top hat and a frocktail coat. He sits here in the cradle, relaxing without his silk top hat, dressed in red vest and printed trousers.

Howard Garis wrote completely wholesome stories, and he had a unique way of phrasing things and creating suspense to hold the attention of his readers. At the close of each story, he would lead up to an exciting conclusion, but make the reader wait until the next

Photo 36: Cloth dolls: (clockwise from left) 20-inch-tall "Uncle Wiggily"; the Chase Play doll, made entirely of woven stockinette; "Buttercup," a character from the 1920s comic strip "Toots and Casper"; boy and girl pillow dolls made around 1926; Esmerelda, made in the early 1900s; a black doll whose pattern first appeared in Harper's Bazaar *in 1892; "Skeezix," a character from the original "Gasoline Alley" comic strip; and a Cuddle Kewpie, one of the few cloth Kewpies.*

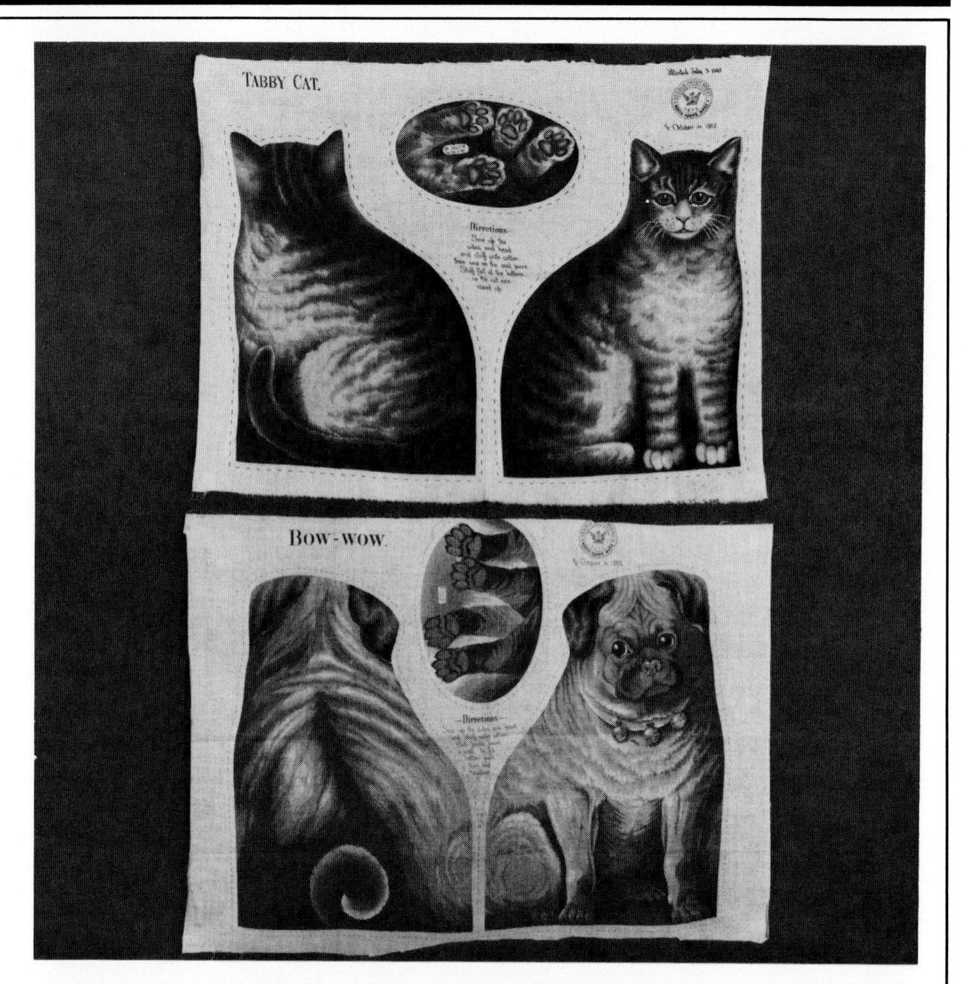

Photo 37: Rag animals (printed on cloth) to be cut out and stuffed, patented in 1892.

Photo 38: Some rather modern cloth dolls are (clockwise from left) Jewell, handmade around 1959; Grampaw, twenty inches tall, fairly recently made by Marti Noble in California; "Honey Lou," made in 1945; "Jiminy Cricket," an early felt version; Sammy, made around 1935; and an 8-inch pocket doll created by Joan Walsh Anglund around 1970.

story to find out what would happen. Each story concluded with a rib-tickling phrase such as, "I will tell you in the next chapter if the egg beater will help the can opener to take the olives out of the gold fish bowl and make a chocolate cake for the canary bird," or "if the pussydog will give the puppycat a ride in the doll carriage down to the corner and back, I'll tell you more in the next chapter."

Each episode began with the classic phrase, "Once upon a time, there lived in a hollow stump bungalow, a jolly old rabbit gentleman named Uncle Wiggily. His last name was Longears." With Uncle Wiggily lived other rabbit children—Sammie and Susie Littletail and Bunty; also Dickie Chip-Chip, the sparrow boy, Grandfather Goosey Gander, and others. His stories often centered around the other animals who were always playing tricks on him and his friends, so they were known as the "Bad Chaps." Some of the bad chaps were Fuzzie Fox, the Wolf, and the Bobcat. It was not hard to thrust oneself into the feeling of the story, for the stories were illustrated in a delightful manner, showing a true bungalow house coming out of the bottom of an old tree stump, and the "Bad Chaps" looked really bad, with red tongues hanging out of their mouths, ready to devour Uncle Wiggily and his friends. Uncle Wiggily's greatest friend was a nice Muskrat lady named Nurse Jane Fuzzy Wuzzy. She was his housekeeper and helped to look after all the rabbits who lived with him. I suggest you treat yourself to an afternoon of fun, by going to your local library to check out one of the Uncle Wiggily books and to be entertained by these imaginative tales.

The boy and girl dolls at the center back of the photo are 12-inch tall pillow dolls, made from a pattern stamped for embroidery, with painted and embroidered facial features and detail of clothing outlined in embroidery stitches. These were made around 1926.

To the right of this pair is Esmerelda, an old, 24-inch-tall doll, unmarked, but of about the same age as the Chase doll of the early 1900s. It is entirely made from cloth, with painted facial features and hair, and cloth arms and legs with stitched fingers and toes. She is dressed like an early pioneer woman, in old, white cotton dress and red gingham sunbonnet.

The black cloth doll next to Esmerelda is 11 inches tall and very old. It was handknit from black yarn with grey yarn hair; she is dressed in a red knit jumper over an ivory knit blouse. The pattern for this doll first appeared in *Harper's Bazaar* magazine in 1892.

By the mid-1880s, rag dolls and animals were being printed on shiny cloth, to be bought by the yard, cut out, sewed, and stuffed at home. In *Photo 37* are displayed two such pieces of material, with uncut animals, by Arnold Print Works. One is labeled "Tabby Cat" and the other "Bow Wow." The patent dates printed on both the cat and dog are "July 5, 1892" and "October 4, 1892."

On the modern side, in *Photo 38* is a group of cloth dolls, some made by well-known commercial designers, but also some that were handmade by homemakers for their own children.

At back left, Jewell, the 17-inch tall, black, cloth doll was handmade of cotton, around 1959, with black yarn hair, very expressive big eyes, and bright red nose and mouth. She is dressed in a red dress with sash of red and white polka dots.

Photo 39: Here is a wonderful, all-felt, 23-inch doll made in Turin, Italy in the early 1920s.

Sammy, the smaller, black, boy doll, has been cut out and assembled from a yard of printed cotton. His eyes of shiny black are exaggerated in size, and he sports a wide, toothy grin. He wears an outfit of blue overalls and holds an apple in his hands. He dates to around 1935.

"Grampaw" stands 20 inches tall, towering above all others in this group. He is 100 percent cloth with mitten-type hands, and a fringe of grey hair encircling his bald head. He has an interesting face with clear-cut blue eyes, heavy grey eyebrows, moustache, and goatee. He is dressed in cotton shirt, bow tie, vest, and trousers. He is a fairly new doll and was made by Marti Noble in California.

At left front is an 8-inch-tall pocket doll created by Joan Walsh Anglund, who has gained quite a reputation for her fetching creation of an almost faceless doll. Two embroidered dots for eyes are all that are needed to set off the otherwise blank cloth face and red yarn hair. The gigantic, black felt cowboy hat on this whimsical doll offers great contrast to the tiny little guns in holsters on the hips of the doll. This was one of her early cloth creations around 1970.

The awesome looking character with tall black hat is an early felt version of "Jiminy Cricket," a *Walt Disney* cartoon character, made by R. Dakin in 1959.

At far right, in back, is Honey Lou, a cloth doll with a rather gaudy printed outfit and brightly painted round cloth face, which was made in 1945 right after World War II, by J. Swedlin, Inc., of New York. During this period, camouflage material was widely used in our army to blend in with the trees and grass, to protect the soldiers from enemy attack. This material is a carryover from that era.

Photo 39 shows the marvelous detail of an all-felt doll made by Madame Lenci di E. Scavini in the early 1920s in Turin, Italy. Cloth was the principal product of this Italian community, and both Elena (nicknamed Lenci) and her husband, Enrico, were very artistic, and loved to work with the woolen felts. The doll shown here is a 23-inch tall doll, advertised in a 1923 *Playthings* magazine as a lady doll. She has the look of Little Bo Peep from the nursery rhyme, with a very expressive face painted on a molded felt head. She is completely original, as are her wig and clothes, and is beautifully dressed in a deep teal-blue, felt dress with fully gathered skirt, which is scalloped and trimmed with a colonial bouquet of pink felt roses. The scoop neckline and short sleeves are trimmed with a roll of gathered white organdy, and she carries another bouquet of felt flowers in her hand. On her blonde mohair wig of curls, she wears a black lace bonnet which ties under the chin; it, too, is trimmed in matching felt flowers. She wears long organdy pantalets, petticoat, white cotton stockings, and black leather, high-heeled party slippers, which button across the instep.

In *Photo 40* we see a plump, modern, cloth frog made from green cotton poplin in 1976 by Marcella Marschel, a Denver artist who calls herself "A Fabric Serendipitist." By working a little modern magic with the zipper on the underside of the frog, the plump green frog opens up and a Prince jumps out. *Photo 41* shows the now-deflated green frog beside the handsome Prince, who is dressed in a regal purple velvet suit with fancy lace jabot at the neck, and a crown resting on his flame-colored curls of yarn.

If you are unfamiliar with the old fairy tale of the "Frog Prince," it is briefly told here. There once lived a king who had a very beautiful daugher. She used to sit by the well and toss a golden ball into the air and catch it. One day the ball escaped the hand of the maiden and rolled into the well. She wept because she could not reach it. A voice asked, "What ails thee, king's daughter?" There was no one near the well, except a frog with a thick, ugly head. She told the frog her problem, and he offered to get the ball out of the well if she would promise to love him and have him for a companion and playmate. The princess foolishly agreed, without intending to keep her promise. However, her father, the king, insisted that she must fulfill her promise. The frog insisted upon eating beside her at the table, sleeping in her bed, and spending all his time at her side. She became so irritated with him that she finally picked him up and

threw him against the wall; but as he fell, he ceased to be a frog and became a handsome prince with beautiful kind eyes. As most fairy tales end, so did this one: the beautiful young princess married the handsome young prince, and they lived happily ever after!

Photos 40 & 41: This plump, green, cloth frog, made by Marcella Marschel in Denver, conceals a handsome, cloth prince inside.

17. Japanese Geisha (Singing Girl)

Standing regally, but with face lowered in humility, is the geisha girl, a 14-inch-tall doll with chalk white face of porcelain, delicately molded features, and stationary dark-brown eyes. She has been made in Japan for many years. This one is typical of the decorative display dolls (often called "shelf doll") found in many Japanese homes and handed down in Japanese families. The body is built up on a padded wire framework.

Japanese women bestow lavish care on the dressing of their hair. Their combs and hairpins of tortoise shell, coral, and other costly materials often represent many months of their husbands' salaries. Fortunately, all these things, even the dresses themselves, can be handed down from mother to daughter, as traditional Japanese fashions do not change drastically.

The doll's shiny black wig is styled to oriental perfection and held in place by fancy amber combs and silver ornaments. Her satin brocade kimono is kept in place by a thin belt, called *shitajime* in Japan. Over this is bound the large sash (called *obi*) which is the chief article of feminine adornment on the kimono. In order to hold it up, a sort of panier (called *obi-age*) is placed underneath, while a handsome string (called *obi-dome*) keeps it in position above.

The training of a geisha girl, which includes lessons in the art of dancing, often begins when she is seven years old. The guitar shown with the Geisha doll is called a *Samisen* in Japan, and is considered the favorite musical instrument of the geisha girls.

To the right of the geisha is *The Book of Tea* by Okakura Kakuzo. This book sets forth the basic philosophy of the tea ceremony, and attempts to unite the Eastern and Western cultures in a common understanding. One does not simply sip a cup of tea for nourishment of body alone—one also soothes the soul and ponders in pleasant thoughts and reflective moments. As early as the year 729, the Emperor Shomu gave tea to one hundred monks at his palace. In the book, it is stressed that, "In all circumstances, serenity of mind should be maintained, and conversation should be conducted as never to mar the harmony of the surroundings."

The two bulbous-shaped little dolls at the base of the book represent a variation of the Japanese Kokeshi dolls; these are traditional wooden folk dolls which have been made in Northeast Japan since the early seventeenth century. Though they are usually "ninepin" in shape, more modern examples such as this pair, which are only 2 inches high, and varying in shape and design, have added an interesting new dimension to the traditional Kokeshi dolls. Their features are painted on in shiny lacquer.

Photo 42: This geisha doll, 14 inches tall with a face of white porcelain, holds a Samisen, *the geishas' favorite musical instrument. In front of* The Book of Tea *are two modern Japanese Kokeshi dolls, traditional wooden folk dolls.*

18. Madame Alexander

Some of the loveliest of the modern dolls, which children today can enjoy, are those created by Madame Alexander of New York. These will be the antiques of tomorrow, for not only are they durable, but they are ageless in beauty and character.

Madame Beatrice Alexander turned eighty-five years old in March 1980, but as of this writing, she is still a vigorous, enthusiastic doll creator with extensive plans for doll manufacture for the next ten years, even though the prime responsibility for the operation of the Alexander Doll Company now lies with her son-in-law, Richard Birnbaum. Madame Alexander became interested in making dolls because her father had a doll hospital in New York City, and after watching him reglue and repair dolls in tedious, time-consuming operations, she decided to make a nonbreakable cloth doll that was a portrait of her daughter, Mildred. This marked the beginning of her career in the doll world in 1923.

The highest standards of quality have always been maintained by Madame Alexander, and she personally sculpted many of the models for dolls. For this reason, her dolls have always enjoyed a wide range of popularity. Some of the most notable ones are her Little Women series, Scarlett O'Hara, the heroine from the movie *Gone with the Wind* (1934), and the current First Lady Series of the Presidents' wives, which are destined to become prized collector items of the future.

The oldest doll in the group in *Photo 43* is "Sweet Violet" at far right, made in 1954. She is 20 inches tall, has head and body of hard plastic, with unusual arm and leg construction, which enables her elbows and knees to bend like those of a human being. Her blue sleep eyes are lovely, and her long, blonde, rooted hair is original. She is authentically redressed in a pink taffeta party dress with white organdy and lace collar, over which she wears a watermarked, pink moiré (pronounced moray), fitted, princess style coat. Her tam-o-shanter hat and purse are of hunter's green velvet.

On the left is 17-inch-tall Leslie, a beautiful black doll made in 1965. She is all vinyl, with brown sleep eyes and dark-brown rooted hair. She is dressed in a blue tulle and lace formal gown, with an extremely full skirt which flares out in a wide regal circle. The bodice is made with tiny rows of gathered tulle. Beneath her dress are panties, nylon stockings, and many stiff crinoline petticoats to give the gown fullness. She is properly jeweled with pearl necklace and a sparkling ring on her finger.

Featured in the center is Scarlett O'Hara, the famous character from the novel and movie *Gone with the Wind*, which has become an American classic. The doll pictured here was made in 1961; she is 21 inches tall with vinyl head and arms, hard plastic body and jointed legs, rooted brunette hair, green sleep eyes, and blue eyeshadow. She is beautifully costumed as a Southern Belle, in a sleeveless, ivory, crepe floor-length gown, printed with pink roses,

Photo 43: Madame Alexander dolls: (left to right) *17-inch-tall "Leslie," made in 1965; a 21-inch-tall "Scarlett O'Hara," this one made in 1961; and 20-inch-tall "Sweet Violet," made in 1954.*

Photo 44: Madame Alexander baby and child dolls: (clockwise from left) *19-inch "Pussy Cat," dating from 1965; "Betty," made in the 1930s to compete with the "Patsy" doll by EFFanBEE: 12-inch "Brenda Starr," created in 1964 after the comic strip character of that name; "Princess Margaret Rose," portraying the English princess as a child; "Amy" of the (1972)* Little Women *series; "Bonnie," made of soft vinyl in 1954; and "Butch," one of the first boy dolls made by Madame Alexander.*

with lace bodice and capelet, and trimmed with green ribbon belt and laces. Beneath her dress are pantaloons, hoop skirt, petticoat, and tiny green, high-heel shoes. Not shown in this picture, but part of this costume, are her green satin umbrella trimmed in lace, and large brimmed straw hat accented with green ribbon and lace roses. She is one of the finest examples of the Scarlett doll, which was made in several sizes and costumes.

In *Photo 44*, we see a selection of Madame Alexander's adorable baby and child dolls. The oldest doll of this group, at left, front row, is "Butch," an 11-inch-tall baby doll. Made in 1940, he has a composition head, blue sleep eyes and lashes, composition arms and legs, and a cloth body. He was one of the first boy dolls made by the Alexander Doll Company. He is dressed in tiny, blue and white dot shirt and white romper pants, socks, and shoes, with cotton stocking cap over his original mohair wig.

In center front, next to Butch, is Bonnie, one of Madame Alexander's prettiest baby dolls, 19 inches tall, made in 1954. She has a soft vinyl head with the original blonde, curly, rooted hair, pretty blue sleep eyes, and tiny rosebud mouth. Her arms and legs are also soft vinyl on a flesh-colored cloth body. She was found beneath the Christmas tree that year by the author's daughter, also named Bonnie. This lovely baby doll is dressed in white organdy with frilly lace panels and pink ribbon insertions, with a softly gathered bonnet with matching pink trim. She wears her owner's little gold heart necklace.

To Bonnie's right is Amy, one of the Little Women series. She is 12 inches tall, of hard plastic, and has a pretty face and blonde wig. She has blue, sleep eyes, and is dressed in white pantaloons, with a dress of white polished cotton under a yellow polka dot pinafore. The Little Women series, based on the book by Louisa May Alcott, was made as early as 1932 by Madame Alexander; at that time they were rag dolls. This one is from the 1972 series.

Behind Butch at the left is "Pussy Cat," a pudgy, baby-face doll dressed all in pink, and probably the most admired of all baby dolls made by Madame Alexander. Her little hands are very life-like, with thumb folded back and fingers curled; her head, arms, and legs are vinyl, on a pink cloth body. She is 19 inches tall, with blonde, rooted hair, blue, sleep eyes, and lashes. The Pussy Cat doll has been made since about 1965, in both black and white versions, and is usually dressed in a blue and white or pink and white checked gingham dress. This is the deluxe version, made in 1973, dressed in pink organdy dress, pink socks, pink leather baby shoes, and a lovely pink taffeta coat and bonnet. She also has a crier which says "Mama."

Next to Pussy Cat is "Betty," 14 inches tall, all composition, with a blonde mohair wig. Betty was made in the late 1930s by Madame Alexander to compete with the Patsy doll by EFFanBEE, which was taking the doll world by storm. Under the wig, Betty has painted sculpted hair in a bobbed style like the Patsy. She is very attractively dressed in her original clothes of blue organdy dress and matching off-the-face hat.

To the right of Betty is 12-inch-tall "Brenda Starr," created in 1964 and inspired by the popular comic strip of that name. She is dressed in a white lacy chemise and tiny high heels, and is in her original box (to her left). She has a body and legs of hard plastic, with jointed hips and knees, and vinyl arms and head. Brenda has exciting red-orange, rooted hair, a pretty face, and blue, sleep eyes. A booklet comes with her that shows many ways to change her hair style. Originally, she was costumed in many different outfits, but the jumpsuit hanging above her is new.

At far right is "Princess Margaret Rose;" she is a 17-inch-tall, stately doll created in 1946 to portray the young, royal Princess of England as a child. She is all hard plastic (head, body, arms and legs) with blue, sleep eyes and a natural looking, light auburn, mohair wig that falls softly over her shoulders. Her outfit is all original with the Madame Alexander label in the back of the dress. She wears a pale pink, sheer, long dress with lace trimmed Bertha collar and puffed sleeves, with a deep ruffle flounce at the hem of the skirt. Beneath her dress she wears long nylon stockings, panties and slip, and pink leather party slippers. Her outfit is complemented by a flattering, natural straw, wide-brimmed hat trimmed to match her dress.

There were many dolls created to portray Princess Margaret Rose's royal sister, Elizabeth, the Queen of England, but the one of Princess Margaret is more scarce. Madame Alexander does not make portrait dolls with faces resembling the person they portray, but instead, she conveys the image through the costuming, which is always authentic and in good taste.

19. Paper Dolls

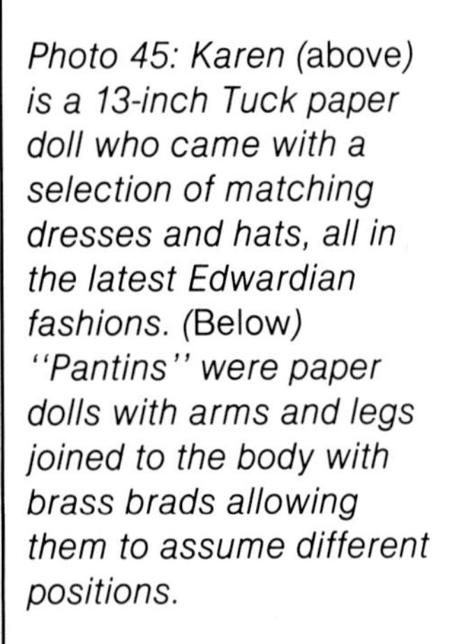

Photo 45: Karen (above) *is a 13-inch Tuck paper doll who came with a selection of matching dresses and hats, all in the latest Edwardian fashions.* (Below) *"Pantins" were paper dolls with arms and legs joined to the body with brass brads allowing them to assume different positions.*

Paper dolls have been a favorite type of doll among children for longer than anyone knows. Being a product which stimulates the imagination, they furnish a form of satisfying solo entertainment for both boys and girls. A single child can sit for hours and enjoy playing with paper dolls, but so can a group of children just as easily.

During the reign of Louis XVI and Marie Antoinette of France, in the 1790s, paper dolls were at a high in popularity. At that time, there existed an action variety known as "pantins"—the legs and arms were jointed to the body with brass brads; they were articulated in such a way that one could pull a silk cord and make the arms and legs dance and jump. Two types of pantins from the 1890s are shown at the lower edge of *Photo 45*—one a young girl, and the other a lady ballet dancer whose arms and legs can be made to assume many positions.

By 1800 paper dolls had been introduced in the United States and were being mass produced in Philadelphia to illustrate fashions of the day, for advertising purposes, and to represent vaudeville stars and other famous persons.

When we speak of paper dolls, one name in particular immediately comes to mind: Raphael Tuck & Sons, of London, England. Raphael Tuck was originally from Breslau, Germany, but he and his family moved to London and opened a lithographing shop in 1866.

Photo 46: Colorful postcards made by Raphael Tuck and Sons (he was printing forty thousand different postcards by the turn of the century).

They were producers of very elaborate and colorful paper dolls for girls, but between 1893 and 1901, they also designed things with special appeal for boys, such as complete farm scenes, boys romping with their dogs, rocking horses, clowns, horseback riders, and fairy tale characters. Tuck also sold calendars and books for children.

Paper dolls by Raphael Tuck & Sons were made from a good sturdy stock of paper, beautifully lithographed, and with several changes of costumes accompanying each doll; but in spite of the high quality paper, they did not hold up more than about a year, if played with at all. Therefore, when one finds a set in mint condition now, it is indeed an item to be treasured.

In *Photo 45*, above the pantin dolls, we see Karen, a quaint old Tuck paper doll, 13 inches tall, with a handsome selection of dresses and hats to match, and even a bathing frock. With that outfit, Karen holds a sand shovel in her hand. You may be sure these were designed to reflect the latest fashion of the day.

A neck tab protrudes above each costume, made to be tucked under the chin of the doll, and two shoulder tabs secure the dress to the shoulder of the doll. The back of the doll, as well as each piece of her wardrobe, bears this imprint:

Raphael Tuck & Sons
Publishers by appointment
to their Majesties
The King and Queen Alexandra
Patented Feb. 20, 1894

This particular endorsement and the style of garments places this doll in the Edwardian period of 1901-1910, during the reign of King Edward VII (Bertie) and Queen Alexandra.

In 1871 Tuck published his first Christmas postcards. Thereafter, he published colorful postcards for every holiday, including New Year's, Easter, and nearly any other one that one could wish to remember. By the turn of the century, he was producing 40,000 different pictorial postcards. In 1880, Tuck adopted the "easel and palette" trademark with the slogan "The World's Art

Photo 47: Esther is a 16½-inch paper doll, seen here with her change of outfits, (next to her original heavy cardboard packaging), made by Selchow and Righter of New York.

Service." Some were printed in Saxony and others in London. Shown in *Photo 46* are some of the colorful Tuck postcards. Top left shows one to be sent on St. Patrick's Day, bottom left is one to be sent as an Easter remembrance; next to it is one for the Thanksgiving holiday, and above it is one appropriate for Hallowe'en time. The other two cards to the right were special postcards of the British Royal Guard outside the palace, and a portrait of King Edward VII and Queen Alexandra. Every postcard printed by the Tuck firm bore the accreditation on the back "Publishers by appointment to their Majesties, The King and Queen," or some of them said "The King and Queen Alexandra." It was a friendly gesture for people to write a short message on the back, address the cards, and mail them to their friends or relatives with a one-cent stamp, mind you! This often served as a way to keep in touch with people living just a few miles away, since telephones were not being widely used at this time.

In *Photo 47*, we see Esther, a 16½-inch tall paper doll in a large frame, which was originally packaged in the heavy cardboard envelope below the picture frame. It is marked "Our Favorite Dolls" and was published by Selchow and Righter of New York. The doll and wardrobe, dating to around 1900, are exquisite examples of the lovely paper dolls which were available to children in America at this time. Undoubtedly Selchow and Righter were competing for some of the Tuck paper doll market. This was a very high quality paper doll. Paper dolls were marvelous style indicators which triggered the imaginations of little girls who could become lost for hours in a phantasy of believing these gorgeous clothes were in fact their own. One can only envy the flattering degree of femininity that is shown in the beautiful outfits pictured here.

In *Photo 48* are the all-time favorites of the 1920s—the "Dolly Dingle" dolls created by Grace G. Drayton; they were much beloved for their wide eyes, chubby cheeks, adorable dresses and hats, and frilly chemises. As you can see by reading the captions on each sheet, Dolly Dingle carried the reader to many countries, clad in many different outfits.

At top left is "Dolly Dingle's World Flight"—from the November 1932 *Pictorial Review*, showing colorful provincial outfits for Dolly to wear in Denmark. Below that one is "Dolly Dingle Visits Japan" from the February 1928 *Pictorial Review*. Her costumes here have a definite oriental flair, with a fan, black wig, kimono, and even a small Buddha for luck. Next to that one is a "Dolly Dingle Christmas" sheet from the *Pictorial Review*. Since the publication of this paper doll sheet, magazines gradually decreased in page dimension; this one was just prior to 1920. It contains a delightful assortment of Christmas toys and effects, including a pony, doll and clothes, toy stove, boat, Christmas stocking, and Santa suit with beard and cap.

Dolly Dingle's "Cousin Lindy," at far right, shown with an aviator's suit and flying helmet, was from the April 1928 *Pictorial Review* and was inspired by the exciting flight of Charles Lindbergh across the Atlantic Ocean on May 20, 1927.

Above the Christmas sheet is a page from the May 1918 *Ladies' Home Journal*, entitled "Betty Bonnet's May Basket" by Sheila Young. This is a beautiful creation of an infant doll, complete

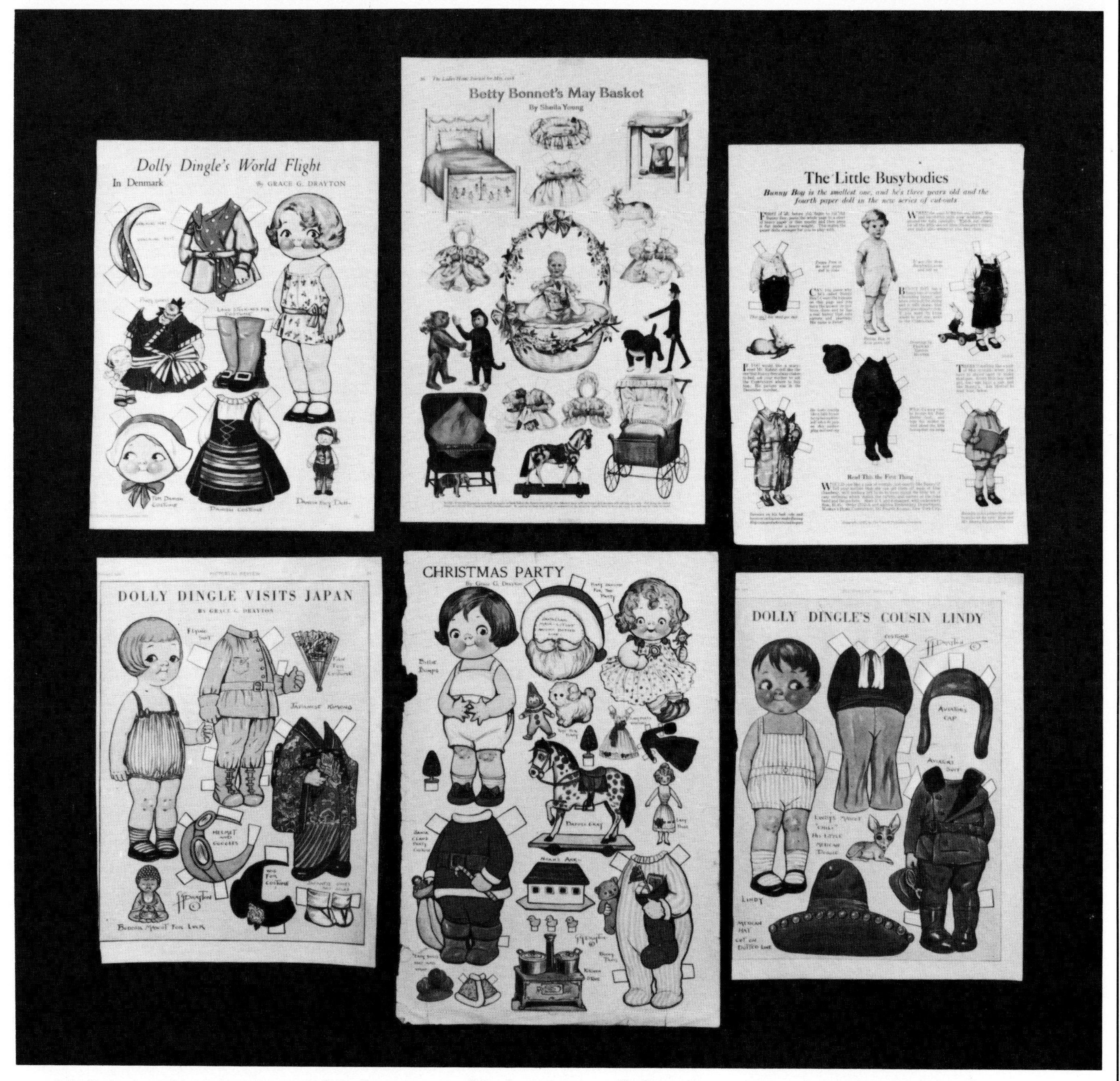

with layette, bassinette, wicker buggy, and baby items, all done in true accuracy of the 1918 designs of the day. Even fashions for babies have changed a great deal since then.

To the right of Betty Bonnet is a March 1923 page from *Woman's Home Companion*, which printed a monthly series for the "Little Busybodies" paper doll. This one was a pudgy little boy with all the appropriate "little boy clothes," and was "Number 4" in the series.

Paper dolls continued to be created in America and were found every month in the leading ladies' magazines, such as *Delineator, Pictorial Review, Woman's Home Companion, Ladies' Home Journal*, and *Good Housekeeping*, to mention only a few. Only two of these magazines are still being published, and paper dolls are now found so infrequently as to be somewhat of a novelty. What a shame!

Photo 48: Popular paper dolls of the 1920s created by Grace G. Drayton and other artists for magazine publications.

20. Dollhouse—Early

Dollhouses have been a source of pleasure for little girls (and women) for literally hundreds of years, over 400 years, in fact. Those that have been preserved in museums, as well as in private collections, provide a wealth of information as to types of furniture and accessories that were in use throughout various periods of history. They give us a visual peek at the life-styles of the people who lived during earlier historical times.

One of the most notable ones of the last century is the one manufactured by Bliss Manufacturing Company. Bliss houses were made during the 1890s and were not large in size or number of rooms, but they were interesting in architecture, with porches and gables, lots of "gingerbread," and lattice trim.

The interior of a Bliss house would typically contain marble top tables, tiny kerosine lamps and chandeliers, since there was no electricity at that time; wall telephones that had to be cranked to reach the operator, upholstered (overstuffed) sofas and chairs, kitchen cabinets (there were no built-ins), and delightfully tiny kitchen dishes, pans, and cooking utensils.

Ideally, dollhouses are scaled one-inch to one-foot, making it simple for a collector to know something she has "stumbled onto" will be the correct size to blend with what she has in her dollhouse.

Shown here is a pleasant little Bliss house from around the turn of the century. The structure is 10-by-15½ inches—a two-story house with one room on each floor. The windows are draped with the customary lace panels. Sitting on the lower porch is a ½-inch-tall iron doll, and on the second story balcony is a metal cat.

Next to the Bliss house is Velma, an all-wood Schoenhut girl doll, 14 inches tall, made in 1915, with a bobbed angora wig tied with a big hair ribbon, and dressed in a blue striped cotton dress. Schoenhut dolls are described elsewhere; this one is placed by the dollhouse to illustrate comparative size of the dollhouse.

Just as we could not survive without grocery stores, department stores, and the like, so, in the case of dollhouse enthusiasts, there must be merchants in miniature to complete the picture. Miniature shops are not new to the collector's world. As early as 1696, according to Flora Gill Jacobs, an authority on dollhouses and miniature shops, a member of the French royal family was known to have nine shops of the market place filled with enamel figures.

In the museums housing the more elegant specimens of miniature items, it is possible to see such things as theaters, butcher shops, candy stores, toy shops, apothecary shops (the early version of our modern drugstores), millinery shops full of beautifully decorated doll hats, and fashion salons. In every case, the rooms are completely and authentically furnished and populated with properly dressed doll figures.

Photo 49: Velma, an all-wood Schoenhut girl doll made in 1915, sits next to a turn-of-the century Bliss 2-story dollhouse, 15 inches high, with an iron doll on the porch and a metal cat on the balcony.

21. Dollhouse—Modern

It would be hard for anyone to picture a prettier dollhouse than the one shown here. It was built by a loving son for his mother's surprise Christmas gift. The outside of the dollhouse is made of wood, painted white, with blue and yellow shutters, and a shake shingle roof. It has ten rooms, including a full bath on the second floor, a powder room on the first floor, and an attic on the third floor filled with all the usual things that become relegated to the attic. The house has a front porch with two steps up to the front door, three bay windows, and a side porch where the garbage can and broom are placed. At the other end of the house is a patio with a long church bench where a little boy doll sits and plays with his dog. The house is surrounded by a large lawn of green artificial grass and shrubs; flower boxes are suspended below the windows, filled with bright geraniums made from painted bread dough.

It makes one wish to be a child again, just long enough to pretend that the dollshouse dolls might be real indeed, and to make them participate in daily routines that could take place in the average "dollhouse day." One could carefully lift the baby out of the nursery, put her in the stroller on the front porch and "play like" she was getting some fresh air for a while, then she would be carried up the stairs again, given a bath in the bathinette, and tucked into her cradle for a nap. After that, the mother doll could tiptoe back downstairs to assume some other household duties, perhaps in the lovely kitchen, which is almost as completely equipped with utensils as any full-scale house.

Now that we have placed the mother in the kitchen area, let's suppose (for dollhouse playing purposes) that she will want to stir up a pie for supper and set the table for the evening meal. Having done this, she will be weary and in need of a little nap herself, so she will trudge up the stairs again, turn down the heirloom bedspread in the rose bedroom, and lie across the bed for a rest while the baby is napping.

At this point, the father doll comes to life in the role of the "fire maker"—he goes out to the side porch and carries in some wood for the fireplace and lays the fire, which will be lighted later in the evening, when the entire family of dolls gathers in the living room to chat about the day's activities.

The next morning, the bustle of the dollhouse begins anew, as both brother and sister dolls arise from their beds, and get ready for school. They will first go to the linen closet with its neatly stacked supply of towels, select their color choice, and take their turns in the bathroom—scrubbing faces, brushing teeth, and combing their hair. Then they must decide from all the clothes in their closets which outfit to wear that day.

Soon they are dressed and bounding down the stairs to the kitchen where the dollhouse mother has breakfast ready to eat, and their school books and lunches prepared for them to grab as they

Photos 50 & 51: A modern, handmade dollhouse.

race out the front door. It's a good thing the dollhouse is completely carpeted with sturdy needlepoint, for I think even dolls could wear out the carpet at this pace!

With the children away from the house, the mother doll makes a trip up to the attic to search for an old doll and tricycle, which can be restored for her children to enjoy. No one *ever* can go to the attic and *quickly* find something, because one comes across boxes and trunks filled with so many interesting old photographs, quilts, pieces of lace and embroidery, broken toys and games; so the mother doll will pull up the old forsaken rocking chair and look through all these things which she hasn't seen for many a day. That is where we shall leave her, with her memories of a bygone day.

22. The Carriage Trade

Little girls have always loved pushing a doll carriage or "buggy," as they were more commonly referred to, ever since the first one was invented by Joel Ellis back in the nineteenth century. With great pride, little doll mothers with heads held high, trying to look "snooty," strolled down the sidewalks pushing their doll babies, and each one was confident that her dolly was the prettiest of all. When permitted to do so, it was even more exciting and realistic to dress up in mother's long fancy dresses that dragged the street, with "klunky" high heels, floppy garden party hats, and carry a pocketbook large enough to touch the ground. All ages of carriages and dolls are represented at this gathering of doll babies out for an airing.

"Sadie," at far right in *Photo 52*, is a 29-inch-tall Walkure doll, made in Germany around the turn of the century. She has a bisque head with brown eyes and brown wig, and a jointed composition body. She is dressed in an old white cotton dress with lots of pin tucks and lace. Her rose colored wool cape is extremely old and has a note pinned inside, verifying that it was made in 1858. Sadie is pushing the latest carriage of the two, made around 1923, of beige painted reed, with two little windows in the hood. The cab itself has

Photo 52: Out for an airing are (left to right) *Mildred, 32 inches tall, who is watching over Mary Marie, a life-size Byelo baby riding in a buggy made around 1915; in the next carriage (made around 1923) is a tiny 10-inch Byelo baby (these dolls were patterned after three-day-old infants) and "My Dream Baby," made by Armand Marseille to compete with the Byelo baby dolls; in charge of these two is Sadie, a 29-inch Walkure doll from around the turn of the century.*

rubber tires on yellow wooden spoke wheels, and even has a hand brake to keep the carriage and dolly from rolling down the sidewalk if they should pause to look in the store windows. The dolls are covered by a pink organdy and flannel carriage cover, with wide eyelet edging and pillow to match.

There are two baby dolls in her buggy. They were new to the doll world in 1923. At this time, a tremendous appeal emerged for baby and child dolls, and every little girl who was old enough and tall enough to peer into the window of the toy shop, was writing a letter to Santa Claus, asking for a baby doll. One that was most sought after was the "Byelo" baby, which was designed by an American woman named Grace Storey Putnam. The Byelo doll was called "The Million Dollar Baby," for it actually made that much profit for Putnam. The bisque head was patterned after a three-day-old infant and looked very much like a newborn baby, even to the wrinkles of fat at the back of its neck. Every lucky little girl who got one held it just as tenderly as if it *were* a newborn baby. The bisque heads were made for Grace Putnam by J. D. Kestner in Germany. The dolls came in many sizes, from 10 inches to life-size and larger. The one shown on the left side of the buggy is the smaller (10-inch) size with brown, sleep eyes, light painted hair, and a soft cuddly cloth body with celluloid hands. Her cloth feet curve in towards her body in a typical newborn fashion. She is dressed in a diaper, shirt, pink cotton christening dress, white knit sweater, cap, and booties.

Another much-loved baby doll of this period was one called "My Dream Baby," which was created by Armand Marseille to compete with the Byelo baby that enjoyed enormous popularity and sales. The Dream Baby at the right side of the buggy is also a 10 inch size with bisque head and jointed composition body, rather than the soft cloth body more commonly made for this doll. Her hair is a soft blonde color, painted before being fired in the bisque, and she has blue eyes that sleep.

Even though the manufacturers of these two dolls were rivals in the trade, these babies nevertheless are friends and are enjoying the ride together in the bright sunshine.

On the left, in the other buggy, is Mary Marie, a life-size Byelo baby, 18 inches long, with a bisque head 14 inches in circumference. She is dressed in a full length baby's voile christening dress with the usual pin tucks and lace trim, long flannel petticoat, shirt and diaper, long white stockings, and knit booties. She is constructed exactly like the smaller Byelo. Her buggy of brown reed was made about 1915, and has wire wheels with rubber tires made to roll swiftly and quietly over the smooth slate sidewalks. It too has a hand brake, and two windows in the hood; both buggy and hood are lined with brown corduroy.

Watching over this carriage is Mildred, a 32-inch-tall doll made by J. D. Kestner, marked "214," with bisque head on jointed composition body, wooden arms and legs, blonde curly mohair wig, and blue, sleep eyes. She is dressed in a long white embroidered cotton dress with double ruffle at the neck, and wide embroidered lace cuffs.

In *Photo 53*, at the left Lucille, a 28 inch Kestner doll, is pushing a wicker basket buggy, 21 inches long, with willow body,

Photo 53: Lucille, a 28-inch Kestner doll, is pushing Minnie, another German doll, in a wicker basket buggy. Sitting in the doll Go-Cart next to her is Angie, also made in Germany.

and 10 inch wooden spoke wheels, made between 1900 and 1914. The doll has a bisque head, marked "DEP 195.14, Made in Germany," with brown, sleep eyes, fur eyebrows, a closed mouth, and cork-stuffed leather body with composition arms and legs. She still has the proper Kestner label on her chest, with the crown and streamers and "JDK Germany." The baby doll in her carriage is Minnie, a 15 inch bisque made in Germany around 1925. She has a cloth body and composition hands, a solid dome bisque head with closed mouth, and is marked "Germany 140014." She is dressed in white cotton baby dress, with hand-knit sweater and hand-crocheted bonnet.

At right is Angie, a 16-inch doll made by Kley & Hahn in Germany around 1913. She is marked "☐ 176-9," with bisque head on composition body, arms, and legs. She has an open mouth with molded tongue and two upper teeth, and a human hair wig. Angie is dressed in a white cotton dress with wide pleated ruffle, and short puffed sleeves. She rides in a doll Go-Cart with seat 6½ inches square, 8-inch rear wooden wheels, and 5-inch front wheels. It was made around 1914. At the time, according to the Marshall Field toy catalogue, they sold for $4.40/dozen!

In *Photo 54,* at the left stands Elaine, a 28-inch tall doll made in 1906 by Schoenau and Hoffmeister (Germany). Elaine has a pretty bisque head marked "☐" with brown, sleep eyes and lashes, and a blonde wig. She has a composition body with wooden arms and legs. Elaine is dressed in a pale-pink gossamer silk dress with

Photo 54: Elaine, 28 inches tall, stands behind Anna Marie, a 20-inch bisque baby doll riding in a folding doll cart that was sold in a 1914 toy catalogue; next to her is Sally Mae, sitting in a very early doll buggy made by Joel Ellis.

lots of stitched tucking and wide ecru colored lace yoke. She carries a gold mesh purse over her arm. Her baby doll is Anna Marie, a 20-inch bisque baby marked "351.15K," with solid dome bisque head, open mouth with two lower teeth, on composition body. She was made by Armand Marseille around 1924. She is dressed in a long christening dress with a popcorn pattern crocheted bonnet, and a wool jacket with embroidered collar, cuffs, and front. Anna Marie is sitting in a folding doll-cart described as follows in the Marshall Field 1914 toy catalogue:

> Collapsible Doll Cart. Frame, 10-½ × 17 inches. Large enough for 20- to 30-inch doll. Made of cold-rolled steel, enameled in bright black. Has reclining back, 7-inch double-spoke rubber-tire wheels, tinned. Full upholstering of leather-cloth, also folding hood; colors, red, green, brown and black. Strap, with hood. ¼ dozen in a crate—Dozen $52.00

At right is Sally Mae, a 15-inch-tall bisque doll made by Heubach-Koppelsdorf in Germany around 1925, marked "320-2/0," with a bisque head and brown mohair wig, blue, sleep eyes, and jointed composition body, arms, and legs. She is dressed in a long cotton dress with pleated front, trimmed in lace around the neck and cuffs. She is sitting in one of the earliest doll buggies, made by Joel Ellis completely of wood with two huge wooden spoke wheels in the rear, and two smaller ones positioned close together in the front.

The Snow Battle, 1912

Engagement announcement, St. Valentine's Day, 1915

St. Patrick's Day Party, 1918

Miss Alice at the Tea Table, 1916

Springtime Fancies, 1911

Married at Home, 1919

Independence Day, 1912

Afternoon Frolic, 1910

One-Room School, 1909

Fall Fashion Show, 1905

Thanksgiving Preparations, 1909

Christmas Morning, 1912

Wednesday in the Sewing Room 1910

Elizabeth 1979
reproduction of French
Jumeau of 1885

23. "A PRETTY GIRL—"

Photo 55: Suzanne, an 18-inch-tall doll made by Kestner in 1911.

Featured on the next few pages is a series of portraits of exceptionally pretty dolls, very choice selections, and all beautifully costumed.

Photo 55: "Suzanne" is an 18-inch-tall Kestner with bisque head on white kid body, bisque arms and legs, and long flowing human hair wig. She is exquisitely dressed in eggshell satin taken from an old wedding gown of 1911. The bodice is fitted, with leg-o-mutton sleeves, and her skirt has a lace overlay. Hand-sewn crystal beading enhances the satin bodice and sleeves. Her lace veil falls softly to the floor in a cathedral train, and she is clasping a traditional bouquet of old, wax orange blossoms.

Photo 56: "Jeannine" is an 18-inch-tall doll made in France by Emile Jumeau between 1880 and 1890. She has an elegant bisque head with blue paperweight eyes and closed mouth, and a replacement wig of long human hair. At this time, Jumeau was considered the finest doll maker, and he won many awards at the Paris exhibitions. Paperweight eyes were made by a paperweight manufacturer in Bristol, England, and they were used extensively during the latter half of the nineteenth century. They had a quality of depth

Photo 56: Jeannine, made by Emile Jumeau between 1880 and 1890

Photo 57: Madelaine, a French Fashion doll made between 1880 and 1890

Photo 58: June, a 21-inch doll marked Unis France

and brilliance which made them especially attractive, as well as human-appearing. Jeannine has a composition body, with ball jointed arms and legs. While her costume is not the original, it is appropriately styled in a deep blue silk, full length, long-waisted dress, with a simulated front jacket brought up into a bustle in the back, with ruffles along the lower skirt.

Photo 57: "Madelaine" is an 18-inch-tall French Fashion doll made in France between 1880 and 1900. She has a flawless quality bisque head with kid body in a definite womanly shape, with leather arms and stitched fingers. She has blue paperweight eyes, closed rosebud mouth, pierced ears with pearl drop earrings. Her blonde mohair wig is the original one made for the doll. She is redressed in a gown of flowered and beaded crepe de chine, which was made from an old dress imported from France during the roaring '20s. The lovely old lace collar was made from a pair of fine lace cuffs, and the costume is enhanced by an old brooch, a single strand of pearls, and a striking maroon colored plume around her head.

Photo 58: "June" is a 21-inch tall doll marked "Unis France." It is thought that the Unis France dolls were made by the *Societe Francaise de Fabrication de Bébés et Jouets* (more commonly known as S.F.B.J.). This was a Societe known to have included Jumeau, Bru, Fleishmann & Blodel, Rabery & Delphieu, and others who were famous designers of beautiful French dolls. They combined their companies in 1899, merging under the one name as above, in an effort to more effectively fight the increasing competition offered by German manufacturers. June was made between 1910 and 1915

Photo 59: Jené, a reproduction, was created from an old Jumeau mold.

with bisque head, composition body, and ball-jointed wooden arms and legs. The beauty of her vividly colored bisque face with deep blue penetrating eyes is complemented by the blooms of magnolia tree behind her, setting off to perfection her lovely blue dotted Swiss dress with lace insertions, styled with low waistline and accented with lace. With it, she wears a natural straw off-the-face hat, the crown of which is completely trimmed with many colors of wide grosgrain ribbon in a lovely rainbow of hues.

Photo 59: Jené is not an old doll; she is a 25-inch-tall reproduction (or copy) of an old French doll called a long-face Jumeau. She was created from an old Jumeau mold by Marian Mosser of California, and she has a beautiful bisque head on a jointed composition body, with wooden arms and legs, blue, sleep eyes, an open-closed mouth, and pierced ears. She has a lovely human hair wig of long blonde curls. Jené is costumed in appropriate pink brocade, with frilly gathers, rosebuds, ribbons and lace, with matching shallow bonnet with shirred brim.

Photo 60: "Charlotte" poses serenely for her portrait. She is 28 inches tall, and was made in 1910 by Heinrich Handwerck and Simon & Halbig, with black painted bisque head, a replacement wig of human hair, and a jointed composition body with ball-jointed wooden arms and legs.

For her photograph, Charlotte is impeccably attired in pale blue, pure silk with a low waistline and sash, with flat bow at the back. Beneath her dress, she wears a white cotton petticoat, white eyelet pantalets, white long stockings, and her original black leather slippers with buckle trim on the toes. Her turquoise ear-

Photo 60: Charlotte, a black doll made by Heinrich Handwerck, and Simon and Halbig around 1910

Photo 61: Mimi, a French doll made between 1875 and 1890

Photo 62: Darline, made in France around 1870

rings have been painstakingly restored to look exactly like the ones originally worn by her when she was new.

She was found under the Christmas tree in 1910 by a delighted little girl in Boston, named Thelma Garland Smith. Each succeeding Christmas, Thelma's mother made a pretty new outfit for Charlotte.

Photo 61: "Mimi" is a 14-inch tall doll marked "A.T." and considered a very special one among the French dolls. It is thought that these were made by A.T. Thuillier between 1875 and 1890. He made jointed dolls with wooden or kid bodies, as well as jointed composition bodies. The one shown here has a bisque socket head that turns on a bisque shoulder plate, a closed mouth, stationary blue paperweight eyes, and pierced ears with dainty earrings fastened through them. Her blonde human hair wig is a replacement for the original mohair wig. Her lower arms are bisque, attached to an upper arm of leather, on a kid body, with kid legs and a gusseted knee. She is properly and very beautifully dressed in an old, ecru colored lace, lavishly trimmed with ribbon and beads.

Photo 62: "Darline" is a 14-inch tall doll probably made in France around 1870. It is known as a "Belton-type," having a bisque, bald socket head with two small holes in the top of the crown through which the doll's stringing circuit normally passes, and the wig is thereby held in place. She has stationary brown glass eyes, closed mouth, pierced ears, and an unusual body of jointed composition, with composition arms and legs which have painted

stockings and high black shoes with five straps. She is dressed in lovely old aqua satin with hand-embroidered pink rosebud edging, and an ecru colored lace ruffle. Her straight brown wig is accented by a pink hair ribbon.

Photo 63: "Elizabeth" is a well-done reproduction of an old French Jumeau doll, 20 inches tall, made by Betty Bright. She has a bisque head, dark-brown glass eyes, pierced ears, closed mouth, jointed composition body, wooden arms and legs, and a wig of blonde human hair styled in long curls and bangs. She is nicely dressed in brown and beige silk, with a tan straw hat trimmed in brown. The only thing old about Elizabeth is her gold lapel watch—an authentic gold watch made in 1900 by Hallmark; it is a family heirloom.

Photo 63: Elizabeth, a reproduction of an old Jumeau doll, by Betty Bright

Photo 64: Elizabeth reflected in the mirror of an oak toy dresser from 1896

Photo 64: Elizabeth, seen this time in full length pose, is reflected in the mirror of the old, oak toy dresser, made in 1896. The dresser, including its mirror and carved scalloped trim at the top, stands 26 inches high, and the dresser top is 7 inches deep by 14 inches long, with three drawers. The dresser set was a favorite item for grandmothers to buy for their granddaughters around the 1920s, and the one shown here is a faithful replica of the celluloid sets to be found on adult-size dressers at this time. Most sets, whether adult- or toy-size, consist of a comb, hairbrush, hand mirror, and clothing brush, and might also include what was known as a "hair receiver" and powder box. Women wore their hair long at this time, and combings of loose locks would be placed in the "hair receiver," which had a hole in the lid, and the combings were sometimes allowed to accumulate for several days. Almost without

Photo 65: Fannie, made in 1875 by Jumeau

Photo 66: Paulette, made in 1870 by Jumeau

Photo 67: Rosalie, a German doll made in 1890

fail, milady would proudly display a lovely jewel box beneath the mirror of her dresser; and so it is here that Elizabeth is about to replace her gold watch in her jewel box for safekeeping.

Photo 65: "Fannie" is an outstanding 20-inch-tall doll made in France around 1875. The head, with its original cork pate, is high quality bisque, with open-closed mouth, brown paperweight eyes, applied pierced ears, and a human hair wig. Her wrists are stationary. The head is marked: ☐ The body is marked: ☐ She is dressed in old clothing—her dress is of lace and mauve striped ribbon with a woven-in flower design. Her straw hat is handsomely trimmed in flowers, ribbons, and ostrich plume.

DEPOSE
E9J
H (inted)

JUMEAU
Medaille d'Or
Paris

Photo 66: "Paulette" is a 10-inch doll of exceptional quality—a French Fashion doll made around 1870 by Emile Jumeau. Her bisque head on a shoulder plate has an open-closed mouth, blue paperweight eyes, and pierced ears with the original earrings. Her human hair wig is also original to the doll and is still styled as it was when she was new. This doll is in mint condition, having never been played with; she is dressed simply, but appropriately, and has individually stitched and wired leather fingers. The head is marked with a red check and a "2." The body is marked in blue: ☐

JUMEAU
Paris

Photo 67: "Rosalie" is a 14-inch German bisque and composition girl doll made by Simon & Halbig around 1890. She is a character doll with closed mouth in a pleasing pouting expression. She has brown, sleep eyes, with painted upper and lower lashes, pierced ears, and a cleft mark in her chin. She has "dash" type eyebrows rather than the heavily brushed ones. She is on her original composition jointed body, and her head is marked: ☐ She

1448
Simon & Halbig
S & H 5-½

has been redressed in rose colored velvet, trimmed in old lace, and her shoes are old, perhaps her original ones.

Photo 68: "Bernadette" is 22 inches tall, a splendid example of a French doll from about 1885. She is in mint condition, as though she was never played with. Her lovely bisque head has its original cork pate and blonde mohair wig, an open-closed mouth, blue paperweight eyes, and applied, pierced ears. She wears a pink two-piece dress with white stripes, made by her original owner. The dress is trimmed with feather stitching, a collar of old lace, and she wears an old necklace. Her pink leather shoes are replacements. The head is marked: ☐ The body is marked: ☐ Although not shown in the picture, this doll still has its original box—a rare find these days! The box is lightweight wood and is marked: ☐

Photo 68: Bernadette, made in 1885 by Jumeau

DEPOSE
Tete Jumeau Bte
S.G.D.G. 10

JUMEAU
Medaille d'Or
Paris

Diplome D'Honneur
Bebe Jumeau Parlant 10 Coiffe
En Chemise 2 Yeux 3

Photo 69: Phoebe, a beautiful reproduction of a "Kissing Bru"

Photo 69: "Phoebe" could be mistaken for her original counterpart, she is so beautifully and faithfully reproduced. She is a 16-inch tall reproduction of a natural Kissing Bru. She is believed to have been made by Emma Clear's daughter in 1964. She is incised on the back of her neck: ☐ She has been artistically and appropriately dressed in orange taffeta, trimmed in maroon and brown scalloped lace with a fashionable matching hat. The original mold from which she was copied was made by Leon Casimir Bru, in Paris, in 1895 when he obtained a French patent on a kiss-throwing Bebe Bru. This doll continued to be made by Bru even after he entered into the merger of several French doll companies, called *Société Française de Fabrication de Bébés et Jouets*, in 1899. Bru was one of the earliest designers of ball-jointed dolls with composition bodies, jointed at the waist, wrists, and ankles, having obtained such a patent in 1869.

Jne 10
CLARMAID
1964

Emma C. Clear was well known in doll collectors' circles for the outstanding reproductions she turned out for many years, from her famous doll repair hospital in California. Upon her death in 1951, the hospital was purchased by Lillian S. Smith who continued its operation, as well as the creation of Emma Clear's doll reproductions.

24. Shirley Temple Dolls

One of the most exciting doll creations during the 1930s was the portrait doll of Shirley Temple, made by Ideal Doll Company. Shirley Temple was the darling of the screen, the cutest, most talented child movie star America had ever known. The doll done in her likeness was all the rage; every little girl who couldn't make herself look something like Shirley Temple at least wanted to own the doll. Shirley Temple dolls were first introduced in September 1934, following the release of her first feature film *Stand Up And Cheer*, in May of that year. Both Shirley Temple as a child actress, and the doll created in her image, were such tremendous successes that the dolls were made continuously for the next six years. After that, it was an "on-again," "off-again" product.

The dolls were made in many sizes and with many outfits which were almost exact copies of costumes that Shirley wore in her movies. There were dolls made to look like her as a baby, as well as two to six years old or more, but the typical and most popular Shirley Temple doll always had the famous blonde ringlets which bobbed and bounced when she was picked up. There were paper dolls, composition, and some bisque, but Ideal held the patent on the design, and produced most of the dolls in wood pulp composition.

The one pictured in *Photo 70*, at the left, is 18-inches-tall, one of the early dolls of 1934, with composition head, body, arms, and legs. Though not her original outfit, she is attractively dressed in a silk party dress with full skirt trimmed in matching lace and red velvet ribbon, with matching panties, short socks, and patent leather dancing shoes. Her blonde mohair wig is styled in the typical ringlets which made her famous. Her eyes are hazel color and she has an open mouth with several teeth.

The smaller doll at center back is the 13-inch-tall Shirley, which was introduced in an ad by Ideal Novelty and Toy Company in the May 1935 issue of *Playthings Magazine*. It was advertised as "the new smaller 13-inch size—a new size in those adorable Shirley Temple dolls—just a cuddly armful for the littlest girl. In replicas of the dresses Shirley wore in her latest picture. Price $2.95." The doll shown here has her original wig and pin on the dress, and while the dress is not the original, it is the proper style for her. The pin says "The World's Darling" and shows Shirley Temple in her most famous pose, with her chubby little finger on her cheek.

At the far right is a doll 18-inches-tall dressed in what was considered the prettiest of all Shirley's costumes. Patterned after the one she wore in the movie *Curly Top*, the dress is knife pleated in red and white dotted Swiss, with no waistline, and ribbons at the sides which tied to the dolls' wrists to accentuate the fullness of the skirt. The outfit and pin are completely original to this doll. The pin is a photograph of Shirley holding a Shirley Temple doll.

There was a period of several years when the Shirley Temple dolls were not made, as Shirley was growing up, but in 1957,

Photo 70: These are all "Shirley Temple" dolls: (clockwise from left) *an 18-inch-tall early doll from 1934; a smaller version from 1935; an 18-inch version wearing the dress Shirley Temple wore in* Curly Top; *a "Shirley Temple" baby doll; and a later version made in 1962.*

Ideal again began to manufacture them to coincide with their sponsoring a series of reruns of her movies for television viewers.

At left front is a later edition of Ideal's Shirley Temple, of vinyl with curly blonde rooted Saran hair, produced in 1962. This one is 14 inches tall. These are not her original clothes, but she is dressed in a red and white cotton dress trimmed in red ribbon with a pearl bracelet and red, hair bow.

The baby doll in the front row was advertised by Ideal Novelty & Toy Company in the September 1935 issue of *Playthings Magazine*, as follows:

> Shirley Temple Baby Doll
> Shirley at 2! New double-action eyes with real eyelashes that flash, sparkle, sleep and flirt. Adorable dress, underwear, socks, moccasins, bonnet. Kapoc stuffed body, composition head, arms and legs. Cry voice. 6 sizes. $3 to $11 retail.

The dress and bonnet shown with this one are not the original ones, but are of white cotton, hand-smocked in pink and blue. There were not too many of the baby dolls made, so this is a rather rare find for doll collectors.

25. Music Box Toys

Photo 71: Three modern music boxes carved and painted by Robert J. Smith of Colorado.

Since a limited number of people are endowed with talent for playing a musical instrument, mankind, since ancient days, has had to rely on listening to some kind of mechanical instrument which requires no knowledge of music in order to play it. Ingenious inventors have given us many conveyances for this purpose, such as Edison's "gramophone," the radio, the "juke box" of the 1940s, and the television, which, in itself, has made tremendous progress since 1950.

One of the oldest forms of mechanical musical instruments, which is still bringing pleasure to adults, as well as to children, is the music box. Toy music boxes were introduced first in Geneva, Switzerland, late in the eighteenth century. The fan-disc movements were made in Switzerland, and the cases were at that time mostly gold and silver snuff boxes which were made in London, France, and Glasgow. In 1810, David Le Coultre of Geneva, a member of a famous watch-making family, applied the brass cylinder to the music box to make the cylinder play music from musical teeth arranged parallel to each other. This is in general the same type of mechanism used in our music boxes today.

Shown in *Photos 71, 72,* and *73* are some very unique modern music boxes, all hand-carved and painted by Robert J. Smith, a well-known wood carver from Colorado. His designs are original and cleverly executed with a great feeling of imagination, and most pieces are mechanized so that the scenes move in an animated way.

Photo 71 is a grouping of three very interesting ones, easily recognizable for what they depict. The intricate Ferris Wheel at the

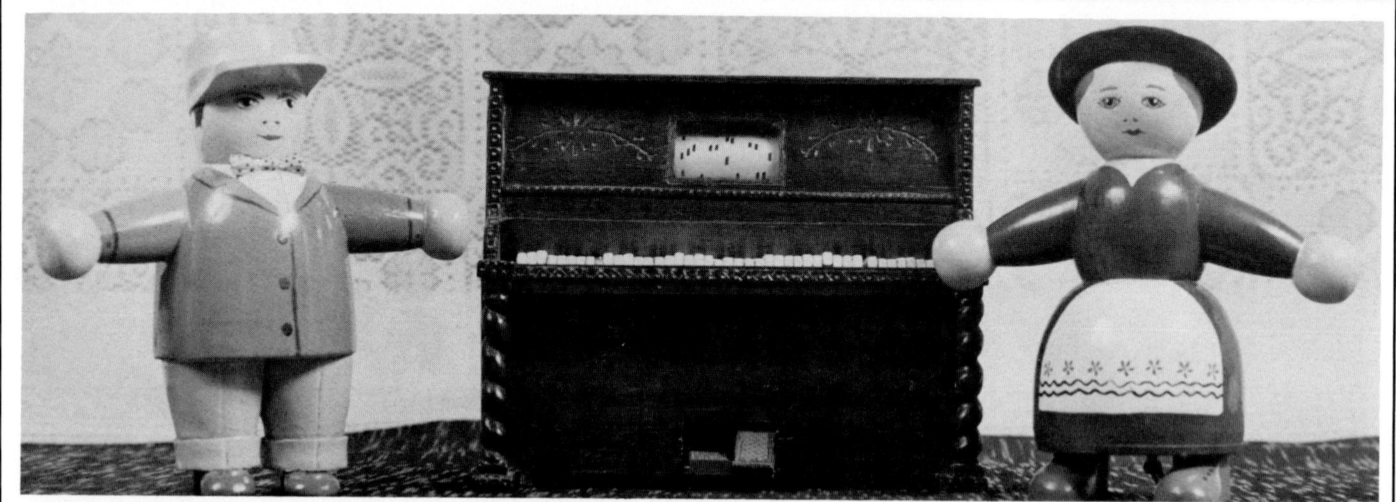

Photo 72: Hildy and Fritz, and a player piano (also by R. Smith)

Photo 73: More musical toys (by R. Smith)

left moves as lively as any you have seen at the carnival, and each of the swinging seats moves as well. Its music box plays "Stardust." The scene portrayed in the center of the picture is of a carved wooden dog in a shop window, and its music box plays (could you have guessed?) "How Much Is That Doggy In The Window?" The title of the one at the right is "Sharpening the Axe." A stoop-shouldered man sitting at the blade sharpener is getting the axe ready to deal with the rooster at the right, who has an expression of fear and apprehension on his face. The tune in this music box is quite appropriate: "*Auf Wiedersehn.*"

Photo 72 might have been taken directly from a German beer garden back in 1925. Hildy and Fritz, a "hefty" German pair, are standing by a player piano. The piano roll moves and the foot pedals keep time to the melodious "Viennese Waltz." Hildy's music box plays the "Blue Danube Waltz," and Fritz's plays the tune "Oh, Mein Papa."

Photo 73 is a group of clowns and a rocking horse. The single clown at left is a typical hobo clown, whose music box plays

"Laugh, Clown, Laugh." The acrobat clowns at right, when wound, do a synchronized tumbling act with one flipping over while the other remains upright. Their tune is "Carnival of Venice." The rocking horse is 9 inches high, and 10 inches overall in length. His coat is dappled gray, and his tail was once a piece of clothesline. He is handsomely saddled and bridled with a genuine leather saddle with wooden stirrups. He looks sharply ahead with stationary brown glass eyes. His tune? "Rockabye Baby!"

Photo 74: Music box toys: house with mill wheel (left) and house with reindeer, both by R. Smith; mother and baby; made in Switzerland

Photo 74: Only one of this group is made commercially. The scene depicts a mother about to pick up her baby, or perhaps she is just going to rock it. The platform on which she stands revolves as the music box plays "Brahms Lullaby." This one was made in Switzerland by Anri, with a Reuge Swiss musical movement.

The other two music boxes in *Photo 74* were done by Bob Smith. It is not hard to recognize "Rudolph, the Red-Nosed Reindeer," perched above the Swiss chalet. As his music box sings out that tune, Rudolph soars in a circle around the house top. The other music box is in an Irish setting—a neat little village house, with a weather vein above its chimney, a mill wheel and a stream in front, and a tiny figure of a postman is walking across the footbridge, with a sack of mail over his back. This music box plays "Tipperary" and "Wearing of the Green." If your eye is searching for the key to wind this one, it will elude you, for Mr. Smith has cleverly hidden its winding gears inside the old mill wheel, where a twist of the wheel initiates the music box tunes.

26. Fun in the Snow

Gussie, with snowball in hand, is ready to wage a serious snow battle on a bright wintry day. Even though it is cold and crisp outdoors, he is warmly dressed for vigorous play before retreating indoors. Gussie and his friends are riding on an old wooden sled with iron runners, made around 1900. There is a freshly laid blanket of snow by the creek, and the puffy undisturbed banks of snow near the sled look like nature's own marshmallow treats.

Gussie is a 14-inch character baby, with a beautiful bisque head on a bent-leg composition body with blonde wig in a boyish bob. He has a delightfully impish face with blue eyes that sleep, and he was made in Germany around 1912 by J.D. Kestner. Gussie is dressed in a two-piece ivory colored wool flannel coat, and leggings with three buttons and a strap that fits under his shoe. To keep him extra warm, he wears a blue and white striped knit stocking cap with matching scarf and little mittens.

The little fellow in the middle is Mickey, a 10-inch "Dream Baby" made in 1924 by Armand Marseille in Germany to be sold in the United States by the Arranbee Doll Company. (*See The Carriage Trade* chapter also). Mickey has a bisque head with a bent-leg composition body, and he is dressed in a knit ivory colored "pram" suit with matching cap, trimmed in blue ribbons and embroidered flowers.

Susie, at right, is a 14-inch doll, again with the bisque head on a bent-leg composition body. She has blue, sleep eyes and a brown bobbed wig with bangs. She was made around 1910 by Heubach of Koppelsdorf of Germany. She is called a "breather" because she has pierced nostrils to make her appear more real looking. Susie is dressed in a blue and white patterned sweater and leggings with a matching stocking cap.

The shadows are getting longer and the creek back of this trio is just short of freezing, so it will not be long before they must jump off the sled and make tracks toward the house to get warm.

Photo 75: Gussie, Mickey and Susie are having fun on an old, wooden sled made around 1900.

27. Cocoa Party

Gussie, Susie, and Mickey finally got chilled and have come into the house where they will be joined by other friends who have been invited to play with them. Mickey, who is the baby of the three, has been tucked into his cradle for a nap.

Gussie and Susie are shown at the table enjoying a nice steaming cup of warm cocoa with their friends. With his "wraps" off, Gussie now wears a blue and white striped romper suit and white socks with little black leather shoes that tie. Susie has on a little pink silk dress with embroidery and lace trim, matching panties, and a pink bow in her hair. She wants to be certain that Gussie will take notice of her. See how closely she snuggles up to him?

Peter, at the back of the table, is an 18-inch bent-leg character baby with a bisque head on a jointed composition body, made in 1912 by J.D. Kestner. He is marked on the back of his neck "JDK 211." He has blue, sleep eyes and a brown mohair, short bobbed wig. Peter wears a blue checked romper suit trimmed in ric rac braid.

Willie, at right, is an 18-inch boy doll with a bisque head, lovely painted hair, blue, sleep eyes, and bisque arms and legs on a composition body. He was made in 1919 by Averill Manufacturing Company. He is marked "Copy. by Georgene Averill 1003/3652/4." He is neatly dressed in a hand-knit romper suit of beige and green, and he holds his cap in his hand.

The toy doll dishes are porcelain, of a hazy blue and white with gold band. They are unmarked, but probably made in Germany around 1910. The table is set with a round linen cut-work embroidery tea cloth with lace inserts and lace edging, made around 1925.

Playing outdoors in the biting cold air has made all the dolls "hungry as bears," and before you can say "JACK ROBINSON," the graham crackers and cocoa will all disappear!

Photo 76: After playing in the snow, (left to right) Susie, Gussie, Peter and Willie are enjoying some hot cocoa.

28. St. Valentine's Day

Photo 77: On Valentine's Day, 1915, Edward and Peggy announce their engagement.

It is February 14, 1915, and Edward and Peggy are announcing their engagement on Valentine's Day. This romantic pair holds hands in a colorful February setting, by a round table covered with a red cloth and centerpiece of violets in a silver vase. They are admiring the lovely old sentimental Valentines which, at that time, were so elaborately designed to convey the wishes of love from sweetheart to sweetheart. Edward holds in his hand a red satin, heart-shaped box which usually would be filled with mouth-watering chocolates and that is what Peggy *thinks* he has for her.

However, she is in for a great surprise, as Edward has very cleverly hidden a diamond engagement ring inside the tissues of the box!

The captivating Victorian Valentine hanging on the wall behind them dates back to about 1900. It is lavishly embossed with Cupids, hearts, and flowers. The ones on the table (about 1915) are the kind that fold flat to fit into an envelope, and when opened by the receiver, they fall forward into two or three varying levels with lots of paper lace frills, and with very sentimental verses, as shown in *Photos 77* and *78*.

Edward is a most unusual boy doll from about 1915, unmarked, with a bisque-quality composition head with painted features, composition hands, and cloth body. He stands 24 inches tall, has painted blue eyes, and a brown mohair wig. Edward is attired in very dapper fashion in black trousers, white shirt, vest, and red cutaway coat.

Peggy, a 23-inch-tall doll, was manufactured around 1914. Her lovely bisque socket head is by Gebruder Krauss, another German doll maker of the mid-to-late nineteenth century. She has a ball-jointed composition body with wooden hands, probably made by Heinrich Handwerck. Socket head means that the head is fitted down inside the neck opening of the body in such a way that the head can be turned in any direction. She wears her original wig of human hair in long black curls. Peggy is dressed in her original clothes of white handkerchief batiste trimmed with many tiny tucks and old lace insertions, with the appropriate undergarments, long white cotton stockings, and white buckle-trimmed slippers.

Supposedly, St. Valentine's Day had its origin in 270 A.D. when a Roman priest named Valentine refused to renounce Christianity and was executed on February 14, leaving behind a note for his jailer's daughter, which he signed "From Your Valentine." Valentines have been found to convey messages of love in Europe back to the eighteenth century and were imported to the United States for many years. Raphael Tuck was one of the leading producers of these beautiful valentines. About 200 years later, lovely handmade lace ones were created in the U.S. by Esther Howland, and these greetings have been produced commercially here ever since by all the leading greeting card designers.

Photo 78 is a selection of several of the lacy, sentimental, old Valentine favorites from years past. Some of these are from the 1910-1915 period, but some of the paper lace and three-dimensional mechanicals go back to the 1890s. The one in the middle of *Row 1* at left is handmade and dated 1890, with faded old pink satin ribbon and colorful lithographed stickers. The verse, written in pencil, says:

When friendship or love
Our sympathies move,
When truth in a glance should appear,
The lips may beguile
With a dimple or smile,
But the test of affection's a tear.

It belonged to the author's grandmother, who lived to be 100 years old.

Some of the other verses on the sentimental valentines read as follows:

Think of Me

In after years, when you recall
The days of pleasure past,
And think of joyous hours, and all
Have flown away so fast;
When some forgotten air you hear
Brings back past scenes to thee,
And gently claims your
listening ear—
Keep one kind thought for me.

I have a message, dear, for you;
I say it boldly, for it's true:
One who sent me loves you well!
That is what I've come to tell.

At the right, in the composite picture, are three of the humorous Valentines which hang by a ribbon or have cardboard stands on the back. The hanging one says, "I cannot bear to lose you. Won't you be my Honey?"

The verse inside the square lace Valentine says:

You can make me happy
With one gentle tone
Nevermore to wander
True to you alone.

The heart-shaped lace one has a verse inside as follows:

With Love and Devotion

Sunny be thy springtime fair
with sweetest flowers
Brighter yet thy summer
with its golden hours
And when autumn's twilight
round thy path is drawn
Hope be near to whisper of
a fairer dawn.

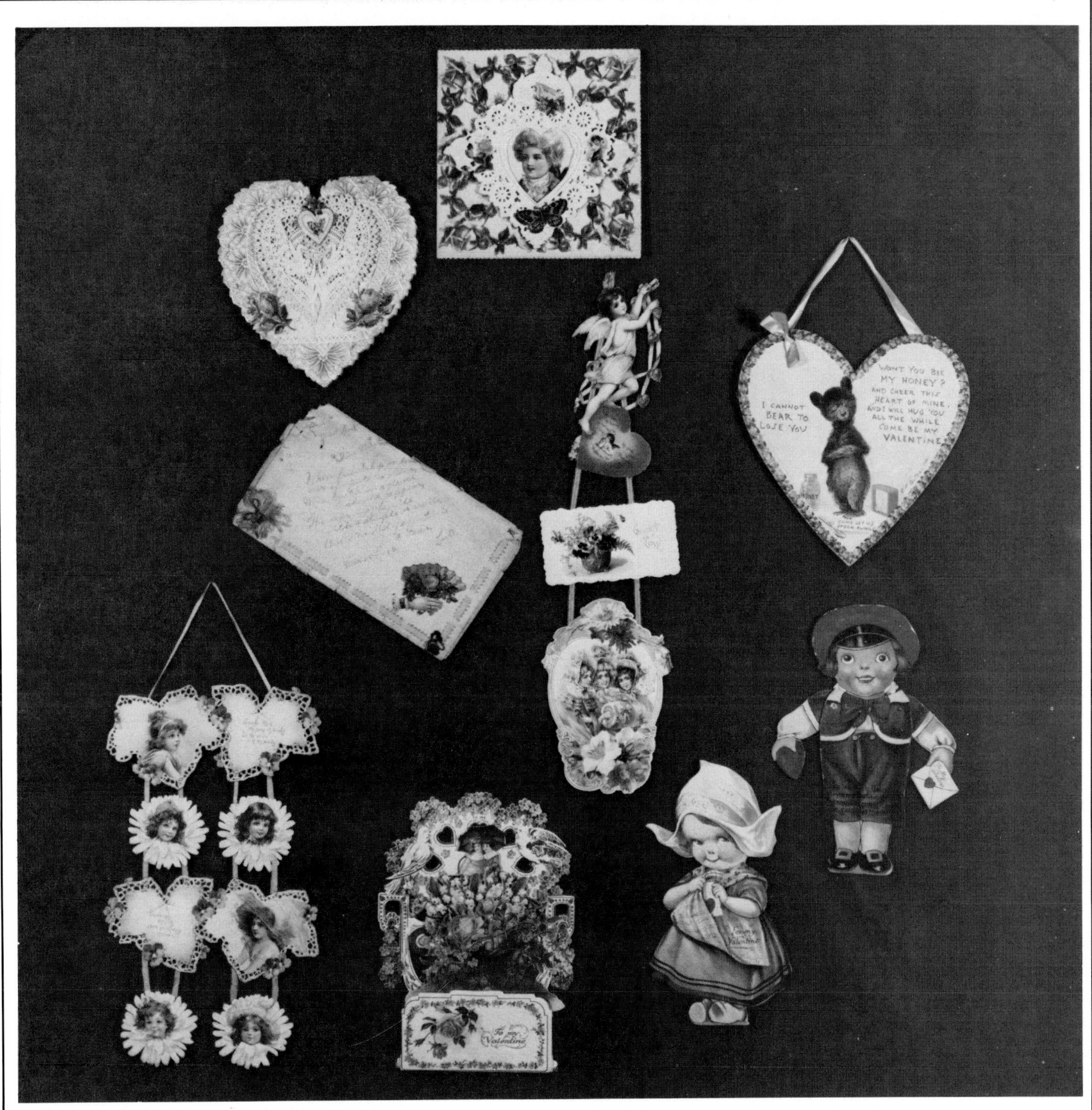

Photo 78: Lacy Valentines from 1890–1915

Photo 79: Edward and Peggy with their "first-born," Dolly.

In the next picture, Edward and Peggy are posing a year after their marriage, showing off their "first-born." They are taking Dolly for a stroll through the park, in a semicollapsible doll cart from about 1918. It is 19 inches tall and 14 inches long, with steel frame and metal wheels, the seat and back made of leather cloth, and a leather cloth canopy can be fitted into the metal frame to shade Dolly's face. The shallow trough at the front served as a convenient place to lay parcels and dolly's bottle.

Dolly was made by the German doll manufacturer, Gebruder Heubach, around 1910. Her bisque head has a closed mouth, brown eyes that sleep, and a jointed, bent-leg, composition body. When not in a sitting position, she stretches out to 14 inches in length. She has a blonde mohair wig, softly curled, and is dressed in a lovely old white cotton eyelet christening dress. Underneath her dress is an old flannel petticoat with fancy knit lace at the hem, a diaper, white stockings and pink booties, cap and sweater.

Edward and Peggy are prosperous, and Peggy looks very dignified and well dressed in her new black caracul fur cape with genuine mink fur collar and pink shirred satin hat with black ostrich plume. She carries a pink beaded purse. Her cape is lined with pink taffeta which even has a tiny pocket where she may carry a handkerchief. Edward's outfit is complete with black silk top hat, a mark of distinction and symbol of his success. They are a handsome family, don't you agree?

29. Dating Game

Photo 80: Colleen and Michael listen to a toy Victrola (made between 1900 and 1910) on St. Patrick's Day.

In 1920, or around that time, one of the most enjoyable pastimes for young people was to dance to the music of the "phonograph" in the family parlor. This was the earlier counterpart of what is now known as the "High-Fi," "Stereo," or record player. Everyone who could afford one had a *Victrola* with all the latest records, and nearly all teenage boys and girls listened to the music and memorized the words to the latest "hits." A girl would invite the boy she liked to come over to her house for an evening (chaperoned by her parents). They would roll up the rug in the "sitting room" and dance to the music of the records.

Such is the setting in this picture, where Colleen and Michael are having a St. Patrick's Day party. Several other couples have been invited to come over and dance all the latest steps with them. One of the popular dances then was called the "Fox Trot"; another was the "One-Step"; then there was "The Charleston," a bouncy, swinging step which *everyone* did.

The parlor has been decorated with green shamrocks and St. Patrick's Day postcards pinned to the lace window curtains. Michael has rolled up the rug and is ready to crank out some peppy tunes on the toy *Phonograph* which was made in the U.S.A. between

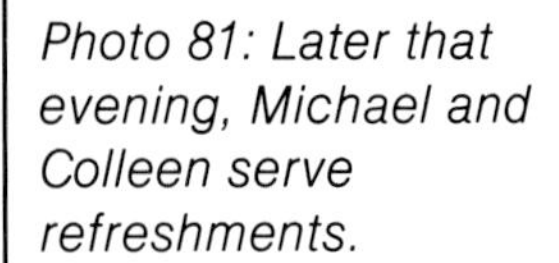
Photo 81: Later that evening, Michael and Colleen serve refreshments.

1900 and 1910, probably by Garford Manufacturing Company in Elyria, Ohio. It is 18 inches high and made of wood and tin. It has a number of 6-inch records which could be played by winding the mechanism with the handle coming out of the right side of the phonograph.

Colleen is a 25-inch-tall German doll marked "Lilly," with bisque head, blue, sleep eyes, kid body, bisque lower arms, and blonde curly wig. She wears an exquisite floor-length dress of ivory pure silk, with delicate French Val lace skirt trimmed with rolled silk roses. She was manufactured for George Borgfeldt Company in Berlin around 1913.

Michael is 25 inches tall, with bisque socket head, marked "Taft 1910," on jointed composition body with blue, sleep eyes, and straight bobbed (replacement) wig. This doll was made by Cuno & Otto Dressel who made dolls between 1873 and 1930. The numbers 1910 might indicate that the doll was made in that year, though not necessarily so, but in any case, it was made shortly after the turn of the century. He is dressed in semiformal black attire with white shirt, plaid vest, and green bow tie.

Later in the evening (but no later than 10 p.m., for it was not considered discreet for young people to be out later than that), the guests will be served refreshments as shown in the next photograph, at the table with doll-size, cut glass punch bowl and cups in "Tulip and Honeycomb" pattern, and a pewter basket filled with green mints. The crystal candelabra are aglow with green candles, casting interesting reflections, and creating an atmosphere of bright festivity. Both the punch set and the candelabra were made in the U.S.A. around 1910 to 1915. The white linen doily with deep crocheted border was made by Helen Boulton Schneider in 1923.

30. The Dolls' Tea Party

Photo 82: Invited to a tea party, Polly and Violet are ready to go. Polly has a bisque head and papier mache body, and Violet has a bisque head with a composition body and wooden arms and legs.

Polly and Violet have been invited to an afternoon tea party, and their mothers have made them sit quietly on their chairs until time to go to the tea, so as to keep their party dresses neat and clean. Polly is a 32-inch doll on a ball-jointed papier mache body with wooden arms and hands that turn at the wrists. Her bisque head, which is the size of the head of a small child, was made by Armand Marseille around 1910, and her body is by Max Handwerck. Papier mache is a material made of wastepaper pulp and glue or other ingredients which are blended to make a strong but lightweight product which is easily molded to certain shapes. Polly's wig is of blonde mohair shoulder length curls; she has blue eyes that close, and is dressed in a new blue party dress with a white eyelet pinafore. When she was purchased new, her owner dressed her as a boy to portray Little Lord Fauntleroy in a vaudeville act in a theater.

Violet is a 30-inch doll with a bisque head, an open mouth, and brown, sleep eyes, on a jointed composition body with wooden arms and legs. The body was made by Kammer & Reinhardt and the head by Simon & Halbig. The head is marked □, and she has a light-blonde wig of mohair ringlets. Violet is dressed in a tan colored, cotton, long-sleeved dress with a fancy brown embroidered skirt. She wears child-size white slippers.

S & H
K✡R
76

Their rocking chairs are typical of those shown in *Marshall Field's* 1914 catalogue, both are about 30 inches high. The one on the left is golden oak with hand-carved trim; the one on the right is a

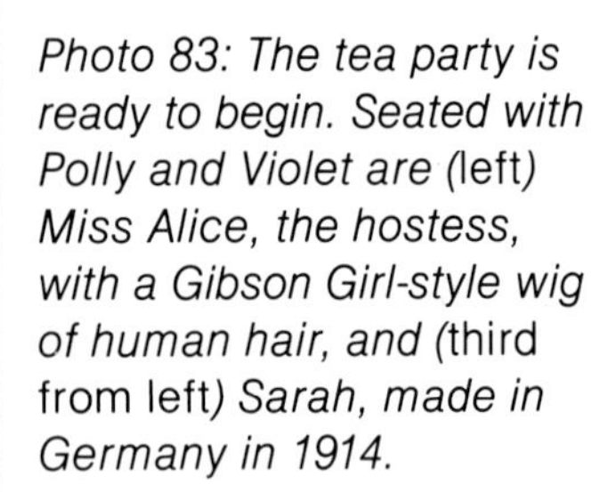

Photo 83: The tea party is ready to begin. Seated with Polly and Violet are (left) *Miss Alice, the hostess, with a Gibson Girl-style wig of human hair, and* (third from left) *Sarah, made in Germany in 1914.*

child-size mahogany bentwood rocker with caned back and caned seat.

It is now 2 o'clock in the afternoon and time for the tea party to begin. Seated around the table in the next photo are Polly and Violet and two other large dolls. Miss Alice, who is the hostess, is a 31-inch doll made by Armand Marseille around 1915. She has a lovely, matronly looking bisque shoulder head (meaning that it is stationary and will not turn), with a long wig of human hair in a Gibson Girl style on top of her head. She has blue, glass sleep eyes, an open mouth with visible teeth, and a definite dimple in her chin. Her body is of white sawdust-filled kid; she has bisque lower arms, and is beautifully dressed in a floor-length pink satin brocade two-piece party frock, with a pearl necklace and a "beauty pin" on the front of her dress.

The other little lady, Sarah, is a 28-inch doll with a bisque head on a jointed composition body produced by Cuno & Otto Dressel in 1914, in Germany. She has an open mouth, blue, sleep eyes, and a blonde mohair wig. She is marked □ and is dressed in a child's white cotton dress with hand-crocheted yoke and wide crochet trim on the bottom of the dress.

JUTTA
1914
Germany

The tea table and chairs are a child-size version of the old ice cream parlor furniture, which was popular in the adult world around 1910 and was standard equipment for the ice cream parlors which sprang up at that time, when manufacture of commercial ice cream was all the rage. The table is 18 inches high, 20 inches in diameter, with a wooden top, and heavy twisted wire legs and frame. The chairs are 23 inches high, with 9½-inch wooden seat, and with heavy twisted wire legs and frame.

The table is laid with a lovely, old, round linen cloth edged in lace, heavily embroidered with a grape and leaf pattern, with doll-size napkins to match. A close-up of Alice in *Photo 84* shows the doll dishes and tea service of china, which were made in Germany around 1900, with a cute design of a wolf, "Puss-in-Boots," and a pig. The set consists of matching small plates, cups and saucers, teapot and creamer and sugar bowl. Knives, forks, and spoons are aluminum, made around 1920.

Photo 84: At the tea party, they are using a set of china doll dishes, made in Germany in 1910.

31. Teddy Bears' Picnic

Photo 85: The Teddy Bears are having a picnic.

It is a beautiful warm day in May, and a den of Teddy Bears, of all ages and descriptions, have gathered by the creek to enjoy a delightful picnic. The red checked gingham picnic cloth was spread over the grass as a casual setting for the bear-size china dishes, from which the bears will eat cookies and honey and drink milk. A ceramic beehive of honey is placed in the center of the picnic cloth in reach of all who may wish some (and bears *always* wish some!). The picnic china was made in Germany around 1913 (maker unknown). The teapot and cups have a scene on the front featuring bears (of course!), and tiny drawn-work white napkins complete the picnic linens.

There are seven cuddly bears in different sizes, made of fuzzy mohair, most of whom are 50 to 75 years old. You would not know this to look at them, for bears don't seem to show their age, unless their owners happen to be "fuzz pickers," in which case they might have some thin spots in their coats. The one in the right foreground with blue ribbon around his neck is a musical teddy bear, and when wound up, he plays a jingly melody. The large one at the opposite corner (upper left) wears glasses, so he can read the "Story of Goldilocks and the Three Bears" (a best seller on the bears' list). There are two ceramic bears—one made by Mabel Oliphant sits on the lap of the small grey bear in the pink rocking chair, and the other one sitting just left of center is the original one created by Ann M. Halladay, who was a prominent writer of "Cuddlebear Stories" in Denver for many years.

Teddy bears have been for many years a source of comfort and joy to both girls and boys. It appears that they had their origin as stuffed toys back in 1876 in Germany, when Margarete Steiff began to make them as a way of earning a living. A victim of polio as a young girl, Margarete was confined to a wheel chair. With scraps of felt given to her by a nearby factory, she put together a small cloth elephant for her first success. Her brother Fritz assisted her with the business end of her endeavor, while she continued to improve on her artistic ideas. When one of her nephews joined the venture in 1897, he designed a toy bear which set the wheels in motion for Margarete Steiff to achieve her greatest success: the Steiff bear is almost a household word in "beardom," and continues to be made even now. All Steiff bears have a metal button in the left ear, which is the registered trademark. Steiff bears were made in many shades of brown. Some had glass eyes, but most had button eyes. All had pointed noses, curved arms and legs jointed on the body, and *always* a slight hump in their backs.

In this country, the popular legend regarding the birth of the Teddy Bear is that it happened as a result of President Theodore Roosevelt refusing to shoot a bear cub during a hunting trip in Mississippi in November 1902. Cartoonists took up the idea of associating a bear with President Roosevelt; subsequently, the President granted permission to Morris Michtom to make a toy bear in his honor. Michtom, of course, named it the "Teddy Bear," and it has remained one of the most loved of all stuffed toys ever since.

One thing known for certain is that Teddy Bears are always happy, never grumpy, always smiling, and willing to be held and loved. Ever notice that?

When the Teddy Bears finish their picnic, they will scamper off into the woods and curl up for a nap, for bears mostly like to eat and sleep, or hunt for berries, if they are awake!

32. Married at Home

As was often the custom years ago for girls to be married in the parlor of their parents' home, such is the case with the wedding party shown here, in about the year 1918. With airy lace Victorian curtains as a background, Daniel, the groom, and Josephine, the bride, are about to exchange their vows to become husband and wife. Each has an attendant; Daniel has Delbert, his twin brother, as his best man, and Josephine has Lucinda as her maid of honor.

The wedding march will be played by Sophie, at a Schoenhut piano manufactured around 1910. The piano is mahogany stained wood with iron legs, and is uniquely designed with candelabra on braces, which swing out away from the piano; the candles can be lighted for special occasions such as this.

S9H
940

Josephine is a 21-inch-tall doll made by Simon & Halbig in Germany around 1890, with bisque head, marked □ , on a cloth body, with stitched leather hands. She has stationary blue eyes, a closed mouth, and a blonde human hair wig. Her bridal gown was made from heavy eggshell satin and lace taken from a 1912 wedding gown. It is smartly styled with a fitted bodice, bell-shape sleeves, scoop neckline, and an A-line skirt with pleated flounce at the hem. Her sheer bridal veil cascades from a flat bonnet, and she carries a bridal bouquet of orange blossoms.

Dan is not an old doll, but is reminiscent of the turn-of-the-century era. He is an original creation made by Anne Luree Leonard of California as the souvenir doll for the United Federation of Doll Clubs' National Convention, which was held in Denver in 1978. His brother, Delbert, is a dark-haired version of the same doll. Dan is dressed in a tan gabardine cut-away coat with brown satin lapels, fancy vest of aqua print satin, tan trousers, with white shirt and wide cravat with a (fake) diamond stick pin. Delbert wears a suit of black wool, white shirt, and wide, black silk tie with stick pin.

Lucinda is a 21-inch-tall, unmarked French doll (maker unknown) from around 1875, with delicate bisque socket head with shoulder plate, on a cloth body with stitched leather hands. Her bridesmaid's dress, of old rose satin, is styled along lines similar to the bride's gown, with fitted bodice, full gathered sleeves, and trimmed in old ecru lace. Her colonial bouquet is made from pink and blue flowers and pink ribbons.

Sophie is 14 inches tall, marked "154 dep 2-½ Made in Germany," undoubtedly made by J.D. Kestner, circa 1890. She has a good quality bisque head with stationary brown, glass eyes and the original blonde angora wig, on a white kid body with bisque lower arms, and with kid legs and feet. She is dressed in aqua pure silk trimmed in old ecru lace, and for the wedding, she wears a shoulder corsage.

Photo 86: Daniel and Josephine are getting married in her home; also attending are Delbert and Lucinda, and Sophie, who will play the wedding march.

33. Modern Brides

In this picture, we present a group of five bride dolls that are not old, but "lovely to look at, delightful to know." At far right is Linda, a beautiful bisque doll made by Beulah Markus of Pueblo, Colorado. She is called a "half-doll" because she has only a head, arms, and body as far as her waist, supported by a cone-shaped platform instead of legs. She has been exquisitely dressed by Kay Johnson, in flowered lace and sheer silk, with a long tulle veil, and choker pearls.

To Linda's left is a vinyl doll made in 1949 by Mary Hoyer. The doll was sold without clothes, for the purpose of being dressed in many different outfits, and was particularly well suited for various women's groups to dress and sell as a money-making project. This one was dressed by the author as a Christmas present for her daughter, Bonnie, in 1950. She wears a fitted bridal gown of flocked lace over taffeta with circular skirt, lace trim, and a tiny strand of pearls around her neck. With it she wears long nylon stockings, taffeta panties and slip, and white slippers. Her wedding veil of tulle is trimmed with lace and caught at the forehead with flowers on each side. Her round colonial bouquet is of pale pink and white flowers.

The 16½-inch-tall doll at the left of the Mary Hoyer bride is Elise, with a hard plastic body and head, jointed knees, ankles, and elbows. She was made in 1967 by Madame Alexander; she has a brunette rooted wig and is beautifully gowned as a bride, in lace and tulle with very full skirt, long flowing veil held in place with a beaded coronet, and she carries a round colonial bouquet with long streamers.

The smaller bride at far left is "Little Miss Revlon," manufactured in 1957 by *Ideal* Doll Company. She is 10½-inches tall, has a vinyl head with rooted blonde hair, and a plastic body with swivel waist. She has pierced ears with pearl earrings and is dressed in white lace with full skirt, a short off-the-face veil of tulle, and she wears white high heels.

In front of Elise is Donna, a 7½-inch-tall plastic doll dressed in a hand-crocheted dress with matching hat and basket filled with flowers. She can serve either as a bride or as a bridesmaid. Her costume was crocheted by Donna Dorn in 1949.

*Photo 87: Modern brides: (*left to right*) "Little Miss Revlon," made in 1957; "Elise," made in 1967 by Madame Alexander; Donna, a 7½-inch plastic doll; a vinyl doll made by Mary Hoyer in 1949; and Linda, a bisque doll made by Beulah Markus of Pueblo, Colorado.*

34. Fourth of July

Why is the "Fourth of July" different from the first of July? History tells us that July 4 is celebrated as a national holiday commemorating the signing and adoption of the *Declaration of Independence* on July 4, 1776, in Independence Hall, Philadelphia, Pennsylvania. Until this time, the thirteen American colonies had been a protectorate of England. The actual writing of the document was mainly the work of Thomas Jefferson, who was only 33 years old when he wrote it. He spent eighteen days writing the famous paper which made our country independent and free. The Continental Congress met on the first of July, and all delegates voted to declare the colonies independent. On the fourth of July, Thomas Jefferson's *Declaration of Independence*, with a few changes, was voted acceptance. Surprisingly enough, the first celebration did not happen on the fourth of July as we celebrate it now, but was delayed four days until the eighth of July. The *Declaration* had been accepted too late on Thursday, the fourth, to permit plans for a celebration on Saturday; and Sunday was out of the question, so it was set for Monday, the eighth.

In Photo 88, "Henry" is pulling his little sister, Frances, in a metal wagon. They are going to march in the colorful parade along Main Street, U.S.A., side by side with other patriotic boys and girls.

Henry is a 42-inch-tall Kestner doll (probably the largest ever made by Kestner) with bisque head on jointed composition body. He is as large as a 6-year-old child and perhaps was intended for use as a clothing mannequin in the children's clothing department. He has blue, sleep eyes, a short bobbed wig of human hair, and is dressed in a navy blue sailor suit, long white stockings, and a child's leather shoes. Henry was made around the turn of the century.

Frances is a 24-inch-tall doll produced by the S.F.B.J. around 1899. She has a bisque head on jointed composition body, with blonde human hair wig, and is dressed in a child's yellow romper dress with embroidered figures, and child-size baby shoes. She holds the American flag as she rides in the old, red, tin wagon which has had its wire wheels wrapped with red, white, and blue crepe paper to show up well in the parade. The name on the side of the wagon is "Iron Clad," and it was made around 1900. Henry's tin horn and toy cannon can be seen at the front of the wagon—they too are about that same age and are typical toys for boys of that era.

The giant firecracker in Henry's hand brings to mind some of the fireworks which used to be displayed at stands along the roadsides and bought by children and grownups in observance of Independence Day. One of the most exciting things for children of all ages, and which one can still buy in some states, was the "Sparkler," which was relatively safe for even tiny tots to hold, so long as they did not touch the hot metal rod after the sparkler stopped "sparkling." They sputtered and gave off a glittering light like

the wand of a fairy godmother. Then there were tiny, little, dwarf-like firecrackers called "Lady Fingers" which were almost harmless; others called "Cherry Bombs" were more dangerous to light and would produce loud cracking sounds; still larger ones called "Giant Cannon" crackers were really designed only for a very cautious adult to light the fuse. There were pie-pan size fireworks called "Pinwheels," which had to be hung on a nail on a post. When the fuse was ignited, it would revolve in a circle, spewing out a dramatic breath of red fire, with a strange hissing sound. There was an innocent little box called "Snakes in the Grass" that contained little pills one could lay on the sidewalk and light with a stick of "punk," and immediately a continuous stream of something resembling snakes would rise up and curl round and round over the sidewalk. There was an item called "Spit Devils" that one had to

Photo 88: Henry, a 42-inch Kestner doll (as large as a six-year-old child), pulls his sister Frances to the Fourth of July parade.

throw down hard on the sidewalk or street to cause it to explode and make a loud noise. Of course, there were cap guns which little boys absolutely loved to shoot, and they pretended they were in the Wild, Wild West. Perhaps the most enjoyable of all, though, were the night fireworks which could be set off in one's own yard after dark, such as Roman Candles and Skyrockets. Roman Candles were held in the hand and lighted, and it was both scary and beautiful to feel the sensation of the charge leaving the candle and shooting out into the dark sky. Skyrockets were a bit more difficult to set off, usually requiring a trough or some device which could be propped against a fence or pole. The fuse at the bottom would be carefully lighted, the person igniting it would quickly jump away from it, and in a matter of seconds the rocket would put on a show worthy of the entire neighborhood coming out of their houses to see the beautiful shower of colors in the sky.

A special treat would be to get to go to a nearby amusement park and watch the special night display touched off by professional fireworks lighters. One would see beautiful scenes worked out in fireworks. One of the more sensational ones was "Niagara Falls." Others included a huge star, and, of course, the grand finale was always the final display of the American flag in brilliant red, white, and blue.

35. Afternoon Frolic

Helen and Della are posing by the water on a hot summer day, but they probably will not "go near the water." Their story occurs around 1916 when it was not lady-like for young women to participate in active sports, and they most certainly *did not go in the water* if anyone was around to witness it. The main reason for dressing to go to the beach was simply to attract the opposite sex and engage in a bit of frivolous conversation, or just to have the satisfaction of being noticed by someone!

Photo 89: Helen and Della on a summer day, dressed in bathing frocks which were in fashion around the turn of the century.

Both dolls are dressed in old-fashioned "bathing frocks." They were very different from the bathing suits we see at the beaches and swimming pools today, but this was the only kind of an outfit considered "fitting and proper" for a young lady to wear on the beach in the early 1900s. It consisted of long pantalets to the knee, covered by a bathing dress, with a gathered cap to place over one's curls, and long, black cotton stockings and shoes. This outfit kept the young miss discreetly covered, and made certain that her "limbs" did not show.

DEP 154—5-½"
Germany

Della (at right) is an 18-inch-tall Kestner doll marked □. She was made around 1896, with bisque head, white kid body and legs, bisque lower arms, and very dark-blue eyes. Her outfit is of navy sateen with tiny blue and white dotted skirt, a sailor collar, and gathered bonnet on her head. She carries her water wings over her arm.

Helen is a 19-inch-tall Armand Marseille doll made around 1905, with bisque head, blue, sleep eyes, and replacement wig of human hair in long, black curls. She has ball-jointed arms and legs on a papier mache body. Her outfit is navy and white polka dot, and she has on her "water wings" in case she should slip into the water. Webster describes water wings as "a pneumatic device to give support to the body of a person swimming or learning to swim." Water wings were pictured and described in the *Sears Roebuck 1908 Catalogue*, as follows:

> Ayvad's Water Wings 20¢
> Afford great sport for bathers, and are
> of the greatest assistance to beginners. When inflated,
> will support a man of 250 lbs. as easily as a child at the
> proper level for comfortable swimming. When deflated,
> it can be rolled into a package small enough to carry in
> a vest pocket.
> Price 20¢ postage 4¢ extra

The wooden sailboat in the water is a model of a sailing sloop with full sails of navy colored canvas. It was handmade by Jim Mains in 1936.

36. School Days

In the autumn of 1910, the first week of September was traditionally the beginning of the school year. It was never easy for the children to assemble in the schoolroom, bringing to an abrupt halt the fun and games of the summer, especially since the schoolhouse still bore the heat of the sun's rays beating down unmercifully upon the roof.

Many schools were "one-room" schools out in the country, where farm homes were far apart, and perhaps there was a total of only 20 or 25 pupils, spanning all eight grades of elementary school. This called for a broad knowledge on the part of the teacher, and he or she was challenged to become familiar with the many subjects covered by all eight grades, even though there might be only two or three pupils in a grade. Pupils in one grade were called upon to recite or do work at the blackboard, while remaining students were expected to be quiet and well behaved. This was not always the case, however, as "boys will be boys," and many times while the teacher's back was turned, the mischievous ones could not resist the temptation of playing little tricks on those around them.

One of the worst of these incidents was when a boy would quietly lift the pigtails of the girl in the seat just ahead of him, and dip them into his inkwell. This usually ended up in chaos, as the girl would, of course, get ink on her dress, burst into tears, and the boy would be paddled in front of the class, while the teacher would be cross for the rest of the day. Another prank that was fairly common was that both boys and girls would engage in a "spitball" battle. They would wad up a piece of paper, roll it around in their mouths, then throw it across the room at someone. Being eternal optimists, they never ceased to believe they could get by with it, but not so, for the teacher seemed to have eyes in the back of her head. She had an uncanny way of looking around just at the right moment and catching them in the act. Usually, the standard punishment for this error in judgment would be that the ones at fault were required to remain after school and dust the erasers and wash all the blackboards. There was always an effort to match the punishment to the crime, and probably the most serious offense of all was to push a girl into a mud puddle, this being punishable by a trip to the office of the principal, where a paddling with inescapable vigor would be administered behind closed doors.

In our schoolroom scene, the teacher, Miss Mattox, is a 36-inch tall Heinrich Handwerck, Simon & Halbig doll with bisque head on ball-jointed composition body, with wooden arms and legs, and made in 1910. She has blue eyes, and a wig of brown human hair. Low on her nose she wears "specs" (a now outmoded term for eyeglasses). She is dressed in a white ruffled batiste blouse with an old brooch at the collar, with a long, navy colored, gathered skirt with a fancy braid belt.

Photo 90: Miss Mattox, is teaching Mary Louise addition while Malcolm sits dejectedly in the corner.

Miss Mattox stands by a doll-size teacher's table which holds her books, a vase of wild flowers, an apple from one of her pupils, and a wooden handled school bell, which she rings outside the door when it is time for school to "take up." It also serves a friendlier purpose, to announce recess time, when the pupils may run outside to play for a while. Our American flag was always displayed and saluted each morning, and a picture of George Washington nearly always hung on the wall back of the teacher.

Mary Louise, seated at one of the pupil's desks, is also a Heinrich Handwerck, Simon & Halbig doll with bisque head on ball-jointed body, and is 22 inches tall. She has her hand raised so the teacher will call on her for the answer to the sum of "2 + 2" from the blackboard "recitation" work. Mary Louise is dressed in a blue plaid gingham dress, trimmed in light-blue collar, and low waisted belt. She has brown, glass sleep eyes, blonde wig, and blue ribbon in her hair. She has on her desk a school book, a pencil, slate and chalk, and a doll-size (salesman's sample) lunch bucket. At least she will escape the pigtail trauma, as her mama has pinned her braids in buns over the ears. Let's hope she can get all the way home without being pushed into a mud puddle!

Standing in the corner with a dejected look on his face is Malcolm, a 22-inch-tall, Schoenhut all-wood doll with mohair wig, made around 1915. Either he was caught throwing spitballs, or he did not know the answers when Miss Mattox called on him, so he has to wear the "Dunce" cap. He is dressed in a navy, wool serge middy sailor blouse and pants.

37. Springtime Fancies

Photo 91: During school recess, Donnie and Albert, 14-inch all-wood Schoenhut dolls, play marbles while Mathew, an 18-inch Kestner boy, is ready to roll a hoop.

In the next picture, we see a happier scene later in the school year, as the children have gone outside for a fifteen-minute recess from the school room. Some of the boys play marbles, as Donnie and Albert are doing; others, like Mathew, love to run and roll a hoop. Donnie and Albert are 14-inch-tall, all-wood Schoenhut dolls with painted features and mohair wigs, and were made around 1915. Donnie, a pouty boy, wears a beige and brown striped suit with wide sailor collar and low waisted belt, beige socks, and shoes. Albert wears a blue and white striped romper suit with black socks

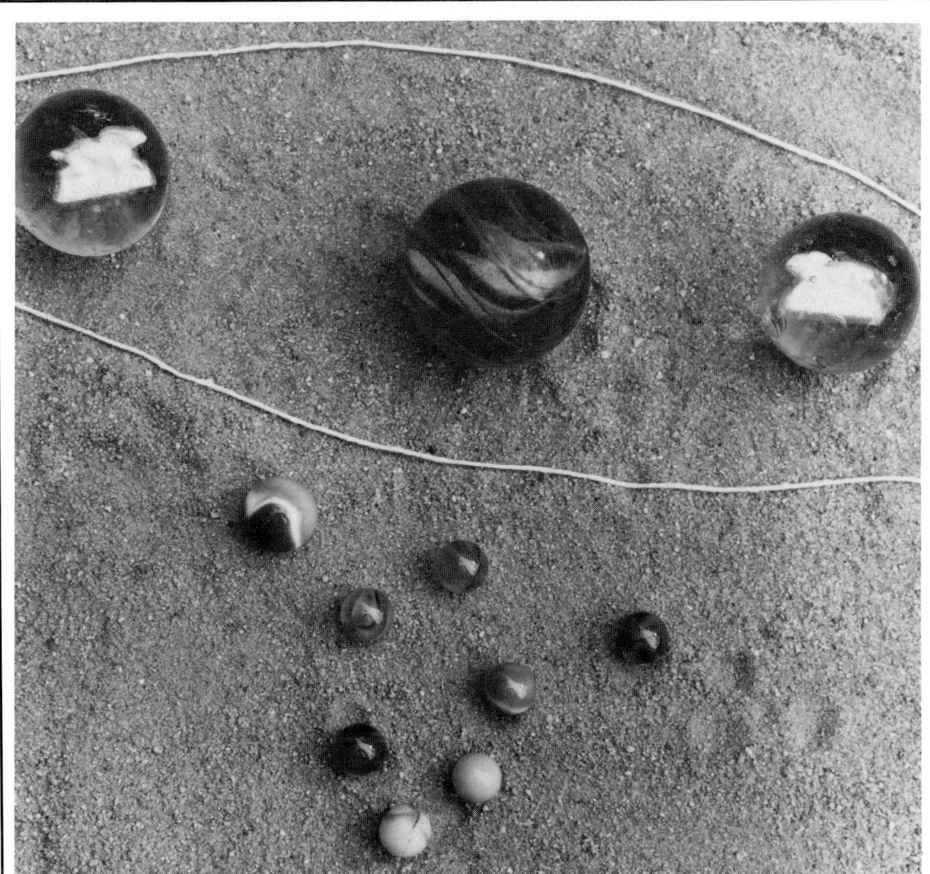

Photo 92: Marbles, regular size and giant, very old

and shoes. Donnie carefully studies his next shot, but Albert seems pensive, as though wondering if he can catch up, since Donnie has won twice as many marbles already.

Photo 92 shows a close-up of three giant marbles, 2 inches in diameter, which the boys will compete for at the end of the match. The two end marbles have a plaster rabbit molded in the center. Regular, standard size marbles and "shooters" are displayed for size comparison.

Mathew is an 18-inch-tall, unmarked Kestner boy with a bisque head and hands, blue eyes, blonde wig, and composition body with wooden legs. He is dressed in a beige and black striped cotton suit with lace collar, and wears a black and red straw hat.

The girls love to play games or jump the rope. Daisy, sitting in front of Miss Mattox, is a 25-inch-tall bisque doll made by Heubach-Koppelsdorf, marked "3025," and manufactured around 1910. She has ball-jointed body with wooden arms and legs, blue, sleep eyes, and brown mohair wig. She is dressed in a rainbow-hued striped taffeta dress with wide collar, and she wears a wire pin that says "Daisy." Her companion, with whom she is playing "jacks," is Lulu, a 24-inch-tall American-made Fulper bisque doll with composition body, wooden arms and legs. Her cheeks are very rosy, her eyes quite blue, and she has a brown mohair wig with forehead bangs. She is dressed in a peach colored, printed voile dress with lots of lace ruffles and trims.

Daisy and Lulu are playing jacks, a favorite old game which is still being played. The metal jacks are tossed to the floor so they will spread over a fairly wide area; the ball is thrown and one must pick up the jacks, singly or several together, allowing the ball to bounce only once before being caught.

Photo 93: Miss Mattox watches over Daisy and Lulu playing Jacks, and Nellie with her jump rope.

Standing behind Lulu, with her jumping rope, is Nellie, a 24-inch-tall doll, with an unmarked composition head, and a jointed composition body, wooden arms and legs, blue tin eyes, and her original dark mohair wig with a barrette to hold it in place. She is dressed in a blue and white linen jumper dress with blue checked stockings and black leather shoes.

Miss Mattox stands over the girls, with a bouquet picked for her by one of her students. Soon she will reappear at the school room door, clanging the school bell loud enough for all on the playground to hear, and recess will be over. Everyone must form a straight line and march rapidly back into the warm stuffy schoolroom, and resume their lessons (or daydreaming??).

38. Fall Fashion Show

Photo 94: In this fall fashion show, these models all have china heads; (left to right) *they are Miss Elvira, Miss Maud Ellen and Miss Hilda.*

As soon as the heat of the summer and the warm days of September had passed, thoughts would turn toward fall and winter wardrobe changes. Therefore, the local department store (usually called the "dry goods store") would eagerly schedule for early October a showing of garments which they had just received and placed on their clothing racks for the fall and winter season. The fashion show might take place in the auditorium of the local high school, or in whatever suitable place the merchants could find to stage it where they could accommodate a large crowd of ladies.

The fashion ramp, as the platform was called, was elevated above the stage and was decorated with velvet and swags of fall flowers. Each model would slowly promenade across the stage, turn and pose on one of the levels of the ramp, allowing ample time for the ladies of the audience to carefully observe the detail of her outfit, and thus be duly "tempted" to purchase it.

The three models in *Photo* 94 all have china heads and are 18 to 20 inches tall. A china head differs from a bisque head in that it goes through an additional firing procedure called "glazing," which gives it a very shiny luster in contrast with the dull finish of a bisque head.

Miss Elvira, standing on the left, dates back to about 1900, is 20 inches tall, and is unusual because of her molded blonde hair, which is styled with bangs over her forehead. She has a lovely face with blue eyes; her head is stationary on a cloth body, with china arms and legs, and she is dressed in fine old lace over pale blue silk, with an old, pink satin ribbon, rolled rose at the waist. She wears a single strand of pearls.

Miss Maud Ellen, in the center, is 18 inches tall and was made in Germany about 1905. She has unusual grey eyes, with a red line over the eye, a mark of a good china head. Her molded hair is black, in a "low brow" style, but her head is slightly turned, and she has china arms and legs on a cloth body. She is elegantly costumed in lovely old black scalloped lace, in an intricate pattern, combined with water-marked taffeta, with an elaborate bustle in the back, splashed with bouquets of aqua flowers here and there. Her hat is of matching material, set off by a black tulle veil which can come forward over her face. Her outfit is complemented by her matching black lace parasol.

Miss Hilda, on the right ramp, is a most unusual doll for a china head, because her black molded hair is covered in the back by a molded mesh cap called a "snood," and she was made in Germany between 1850 and 1860. She has leather arms and legs on a cloth body and is dressed in cobalt-blue velvet, with full sleeves to the wrists, and a V-shaped collar of handmade lace.

In *Photo 95*, the second half of the fashion showing is devoted to coats and other outer wraps for milady, since snow and cold weather are just around the corner in October.

Miss Marion, the model on the left, is an 18-inch-tall blue-eyed doll made in Germany about 1905 by J.D. Kestner, who was noted for making dolls of excellent quality. She has an especially pretty face (bisque head), with brown mohair wig, on a kid body, with bisque lower arms and cloth legs. She models a floor-length red velvet coat fully gathered on a shoulder yoke, with two buttons at the top, and a white rabbit fur collar. Her face is neatly framed in a matching bonnet of red velvet, with white fur circling its brim. She carries a white fur muff cleverly designed to look like the face of a fox. Under her coat she is clad in a long, navy-blue sateen dress trimmed in lace, with "leg-o-mutton" sleeves, and an amethyst brooch. Her undergarments are lace-trimmed pantalets and petticoats of cotton (once they were white, but now yellowed with age).

Miss Helen Louise, featured in the center, was made in 1905 by two different German doll makers. It was not unusual for one company to make only the bisque heads and another to specialize in making doll bodies of either wood, leather, cloth, or papier mache. Helen Louise is 22 inches tall, her bisque head was made by Simon & Halbig, and the back of her neck is marked: "Heinrich Handwerck Simon & Halbig." She has fashionable long brown curls of human hair, brown eyes and lashes, and pierced ears with little pearl earrings. Her body, which is of composition, with ball-jointed wooden hands and legs, was made by Heinrich Handwerck.

Helen Louise models the high fashion of the day: a blue velvet coat with low belted waistline, pearl buttons, and completely lined in blue and white striped silk. With it she wears a matching

Photo 95: *The second half of the fashion show features warm coats and wraps, with models Miss Marion, Miss Helen and Miss Nancy.*

velvet cloche (a close-fitting hat), and her outfit is enhanced by a fur ensemble of white fur collar trimmed with ermine tails, and a matching fur muff which hangs about her neck on a silk cord.

Under the coat she wears an original outfit, consisting of a dainty white batiste afternoon dress with the low waistline defined by eyelet lace through which blue satin ribbon has been threaded. Beneath her dress are two white cotton petticoats trimmed with lace, long pantalets which come to her knee (and quite properly so!), and a chemise. She wears long white cotton stockings and black leather party slippers with buckle trim and black ribbon ties.

Miss Nancy, the model on the right, is a lovely doll that might have been under your great-grandmother's Christmas tree, for she was manufactured around 1891 in Germany by a firm called Simon & Halbig, one of the better doll makers. Her blonde wig of mohair is her original wig, she has brown, stationary glass eyes, and pierced ears with little pearl earrings. Her pretty bisque shoulder head is on a white kid body with bisque lower arms, leather legs, and feet, and she stands 18 inches tall. She is featured in a dark-green panne velvet evening cape trimmed in white fur collar. With it she carries a pink beaded evening bag to match the pink ribbons on her floor length dress of white eyelet embroidered cotton. Her dress has full balloon sleeves, and she is very properly clad in old cotton pantalets and petticoats with long white cotton stockings and black, patent leather party slippers.

39. Dolls of the Harvest Season

The month of November suggests, among other things, our Thanksgiving holiday and how it came about. The very earliest settlers were, of course, the American Indians. Early in December 1619, a group of 39 settlers sailed up the James River to a place called Berkeley Hundred, where they knelt on the riverbank to give thanks for their safe arrival. The leaders of the expedition gave instructions that the day should be remembered yearly and kept holy as a day of Thanksgiving to Almighty God. The white settlers (pilgrims) who landed at Plymouth Rock, Massachusetts, in 1620, from their long voyage from England, first held Thanksgiving in 1621, after a year of near starvation, illness, and many deaths. Governor Bradford invited the Indians to join them. Chief Massasoit and 90 of his Indian braves came in their best outfits, with painted faces, feathers, and tomahawks. A prayer of thanks to God was offered by the Pilgrims, as the Indians looked on in quiet reverence. Later, the red men danced, and all enjoyed a huge feast of turkey, clams and scallops, and vegetables. A day was set aside in November from then on to celebrate Thanksgiving, but it was not necessarily done on the same date in every state. Finally, in 1846, Sarah Hale, editor of *Godey's Lady's Book*, started the wheels in motion to adopt one particular day for every American to observe the holiday. After writing many letters to many different presidents, her efforts were finally recognized by President Abraham Lincoln, who proclaimed the last Thursday in November as our national Thanksgiving Day.

The group of dolls in *Photo 96* commemorates the Indian way of life. The tallest one is called a "Skookum" doll, which was made in Denver, Colorado, by the H. H. Tammen Company and designed by Mary McAboy. The word "Skookum" is Siwash for "Bully Good." The earliest ones made in 1913 had dried-apple faces, but were later made with composition; the bodies are basically a long piece of wood padded with excelsior-stuffed muslin. The dolls represent real Indians of various tribes on reservations.

The tall chief stands 16 inches high, with hands folded inside the wrap of his colorful Indian blanket. His weathered looking, bronze colored face is of painted composition, his body of straw filled cloth. His coal-black braids of horsehair are secured by a fancy beaded headdress, and a strand or two of turquoise and other beads hang about his neck. His moccasins are made from real leather with traditional Indian beaded trim. The Skookum dolls were made in graduated sizes to represent a chief, squaw, and children. The squaw is at the far right, and the child in front of the chief.

The twin papooses in the felt carrier are all composition, made by Indians in Medora, North Dakota. They are very simply dressed in a felt blanket wrap.

Photo 96: Here are featured a variety of Indian-type dolls.

At the right of the chief is "Hoho," a 14-inch doll made by Kestner around 1912 with bisque head on kid body. She has a scowling face, wig of black mohair, and a fringed, chamois-colored suede, two-piece suit with leather moccasins.

To the right of Hoho is Pocahontas, a 12-inch doll made by Unis France around the turn of the century. She is very dark bisque with composition body and straight composition arms. She has dark braids and is dressed in a colorful Indian maiden's two-piece dress.

To the left and in front of Pocahontas is a 7½-inch Hopi maiden, authentically dressed by Indians. The doll is all vinyl with movable arms on a one-piece body and head, black twisted braids, dressed in black dress, navy plaid shawl, white leather moccasins,

Photo 97: Dolls of the harvest season include (left to right) *three corn husk dolls; a cowboy made from a walnut shell; Ana, a faceless burlap doll from Italy; and an Amish couple whose faces were made from dried apples.*

and bead necklace. To her left is an 8-inch squaw doll made from coconut fiber by the Seminole Indians of Florida.

At the far left, beneath the twins is an old metal Indian, painted dark brown, with left arm raised, and arrow in his right hand. He wears a painted metal sculpted feather headdress, and was made close to the turn of the century. The other metal Indian head in the center front of the picture is a painted metal bank, with a very well-done face. The features are strong, and his brow is wrinkled.

Highlighting this Indian scene is a hand-loomed Navajo wool mat made by selected ladies of the Navajo tribe, at the Chinchilbeto School in Arizona. The figures are *Yei* (pronounced Yay) dancers.

In *Photo 97* we see another setting of dolls symbolic of the fall harvest season. The wrinkled face of the old lady in the rocking chair, and that of the man standing beside her, are made from apples which have been peeled, pinched to shape the facial features, and allowed to wither naturally over a period of time. These dolls portray an Amish couple from the Pennsylvania Dutch communities. They are distinguished by their utter simplicity, both in their way of life and in their mode of dress. She wears a sunbonnet of black and a black apron over a drab, green housedress. Her head turns on a wire armature body, and her feet and hands are made from felt with stitched fingers. She clasps a bouquet of straw flowers. Her husband also is attired in very simple black clothing, with no buttons or ornamental trim. He wears the traditional black Amish hat and carries a black Bible in his hands.

To the left of the Amish gentleman is Ana, a faceless burlap doll, holding a bouquet of wheat. She has no features to distinguish her face, but has an outstanding blonde wig that falls into braids; she was made in Italy, and is a very interesting foreign doll.

The cowboy wrangler, with steer rope in hand, is unique for his head which was made from a walnut shell. Facial features have been painted on the shell, and the whole thing has been shellacked to preserve the face. It has been dressed as a cowboy, and all that is missing is his horse.

The three dolls in the group at far left are made of cornhusks. The one standing next to the wrangler is a cornhusk bride, with eucalyptus bouquet, a handbag made from a peach stone, and a pioneer bonnet of cornhusks at the back of her head. The male figure sitting to her left is a fisherman, dressed in trousers of cornhusk, with simple jacket, hat, and pole. A small child doll of cornhusk stands close by, also with a fishing pole, as though it might be a grandfather and grandchild duo. The female figure to the left of this pair is on her way to the well, with a balanced pole of buckets; her full skirt, blouse, cap, and even the buckets, are all made of husks.

Years ago, these dolls were especially popular in farm homes, as the cornhusk materials were readily available and could be moistened and shaped rather easily into forms. In general, the outer cornhusks are shaped while still damp into faces, arms, legs, skirts, trousers, etc. After they have thoroughly dried, facial features can be painted on or etched with needle and thread, and additional clothing such as bonnets, aprons, and the like, placed over the existing framework.

40. Christmas Eve

No matter what age we may be, for most of us, there is a feeling of excitement and one of great anticipation when we think of Christmas. Well do I remember almost a feeling of magic associated with Santa Claus arriving after a mystical sleigh ride through the starry Christmas Eve skies. My imagination furnished me a picture of every whisker in his furry white beard, the reddish glow in his fat cheeks, the laughing creases beneath his big eyes, and the genuine warmth of his smile. I was *sure* I heard the prancing hooves of his eight tiny reindeer, as they slid to a neat landing on the roof of our house. I at least pretended to be asleep, as my mother and father wanted me to be, for I was not willing to risk Santa's being unable "to do his work."

During the time period of about 1890 to 1920, most homes did not have electricity like we now have, and the Christmas tree held many candles which were clipped to its branches, furnishing the only light on the tree. Once each night, and especially on Christmas Eve, father would carefully light each of the candles, but always there would be a bucket of water sitting alongside the tree as a precaution, should the branches catch fire. The little children of the family were privileged to witness the lovely light from the candles for just a few minutes, for that was the only way the tree could be safely lighted without danger of a fire. It was quite a thrill to watch the exciting glow that quickly spread itself around the room, casting wierd but lovely shadows over the walls and floor. This experience was further enhanced by the wonderful fresh aroma of the live balsam or pine tree.

Rose Marie stands by the lovely Christmas tree, pointing to all the shining graceful antique ornaments which date back to nearly 1910, capturing the beam of the lighted candles. She seems to be trying to tell us, however, that the bucket and ladle by the tree serve as a sober reminder that the candles can only be enjoyed for a moment longer; each flame must be extinguished until the next morning.

Rose Marie is a 32-inch doll made by Kestner, and marked "JDK 214," produced around 1915. She has a bisque head on composition body, with jointed wooden arms and legs, a long, curly, blonde mohair wig, and large blue, sleep eyes, with an open mouth and two teeth. She is dressed in a child-size white cotton dress with pin-tucked skirt and a pretty border of scalloped eyelet. A blue satin ribbon sash is carried through lace eyelets at the waistline, and she wears a white bonnet with full crown and wide brim. On her feet are child-size, white, kid baby shoes, wih two straps that button at the ankle, and a bow trim over the toe.

Photo 98: Rose Marie, a 32-inch doll by Kestner, stands by a Christmas tree with ornaments that date back to 1910.

41. Christmas Morning

There was particular joy among the children when it came time to hang up the stockings on Christmas Eve, but the anticipation of those limp and empty stockings being transformed into fat, bulging bearers of surprises was almost more than little boys and girls could bear. Finally, the long hours of Christmas Eve would pass, the children would awaken on Christmas morning, and come prancing down the stairs to behold great workings of magic. Once again, father would patiently light each candle on the tree, the children would sit on the floor and pour out the contents of the Christmas stockings. How could Santa Claus have known that each item was just what was desired? After the stockings were thoroughly enjoyed and compared, one with another, father and mother would distribute the packages and toys that were arranged so attractively beneath the tree.

For the little boy of the family, there was an adorable old Teddy Bear made of a clipped mohair fabric that felt soft, like fur. He had the traditional slightly rounded shoulders, jointed arms (or paws???) and legs, and a little red felt floppy tongue which hung loosely from his jaw, giving him the look of a playful but mischievous bear.

The towering horse is 36 inches high, structured of wood, and covered with real horse-hide in a pretty Palomino color, with light-colored mane. He was made around 1900 to 1915, and was a very popular toy for boys—a real action toy. He stands on a rocking platform, saddled and bridled, awaiting his rider.

In front of the rocking horse is a colorful book called *The Little People's Scrapbook*, copyrighted in 1852 by Ernest-Nister of London, and E. P. Dutton & Company of New York.

In front of the Teddy Bear is a box of blocks that were made in the late nineteenth century in Germany. They are wood, covered with lithographed paper, and they fit solidly in the wooden tray. There were different puzzles on the sides, so that one could work more than one picture from them.

The other book in the front of the picture is a 1912 one entitled *In Cloudland*, published by Sam Gabriel Sons & Company of New York. It was about this time that aviation was having a humble beginning, and books of this nature were enjoying great popularity among boys.

The little girl of the family would exclaim with sheer delight when she opened the lid of the metal doll trunk which was made by Green Toy Works of Racine, Wisconsin, back in 1917. Mother would sew for several weeks prior to Christmas and fill a trunk like this one with pretty new clothes for last year's Christmas doll, or perhaps create a complete wardrobe for this year's new Christmas doll. There would be an unbelievable assortment of panties and slips, nighties and dresses, knit sweaters, bonnets, and booties which would be put on and taken off the doll many, many times that

Photo 99: Christmas-morning surprises under the tree.

day. Every little girl loved to pretend she was the mama to her dolly, and responsible for dressing her to suit whatever occasion she chose to portray.

The baby doll in front of the trunk is marked "K & K, Made in Germany"; she has a bisque head and mohair wig, on a cloth body, with most unusual feet and legs of leatherette. It was made between 1918 and 1920. She is dressed in a white baby doll dress and cap, with knit booties.

The larger doll in the box is a 19 inch doll, with bisque head, and a human hair wig of long curls, a body of papier mache, with wooden arms and legs. She has ball-jointed wrists, elbows and knees, and wooden "stick" legs, meaning her legs above the knee are straight like sticks, while her legs below the knee are shaped and proportioned. She was made around the turn of the century by Armand Marseille. She is in her original clothes, consisting of a

Photo 100: Christmas postcards by Raphael Tuck (early 1900s)

rayon dress, flimsy scrim or gauze petticoat and panties, and her straw hat is trimmed to match the dress.

Christmas then was a great day of joy and peace, and with less emphasis on commercialization, as demonstrated in this scene which reflects the happiness that was found in fewer toys for each child. Except for the more wealthy families, most children did not get, or even expect to get, more than one or two things from the list of things they had asked Santa Claus to bring. There was much more feeling of suspense and cause for wonderment at what they *might* receive, and for days before Christmas, it was an exciting guessing game to try to determine what they most wanted, and what would be decided as the wisest thing for them to receive.

Maybe *these were the good old days.*

Bibliography

Collector's Encyclopedia of Dolls, The. by Dorothy S., Elizabeth A., and Evelyn J. Coleman. New York: Crown Publishers, Inc.; 1968.

Dolls In Color. by Faith Eaton. New York: Macmillan Publishing Co., Inc.; 1975.

Encyclopedia of Toys. by Constance and Eileen King. New York: Crown Publishers, Inc.; 1978.

Here Comes the Circus. by Peter Verney. New York: Paddington; 1978.

How to be a Clown. by Charles R. Meyer. New York: McKay; 1977.

Mechanical Musical Instruments. by Dr. Alexander Buchner. (Printed in Czechoslovakia): Greenwood; 1978 (reprint of 1959).

Spinning Wheel's Complete Book of Dolls. edited by Albert Christian Revi, Galahad Books, New York. New York: Everybody's Press, Inc.; 1975.

Index of Doll Names

Names have been given to the dolls used in this book, both for purposes of story interest and for easier identification in each photograph. In some cases, the name was chosen for purely sentimental reasons to honor someone in my family or one of my friends. Wherever the name used was the same as its original commercial name, it has been so indicated by an asterisk.

Following is the alphabetical listing of names to be found throughout the text of the book.

Index of Dolls

Index of Toys